Side Man

WARREN LEIGHT

Side Man

Grove Press
New York

Published simultaneously in Canada
Printed in the United States of America

First Edition

Library of Congress Cataloging-in-Publication Data

Leight, Warren D.
Side man / Warren Leight. —- 1st Grove Press ed.
p.   cm.
ISBN 0-8021-3622-2
1. Jazz musicians—New York (State)—New York—Drama. I. Title.
PS3562.E458S5   1998
812'.54—dc21   98-54092

Grove Press
841 Broadway
New York, NY 10003

99 00 01   10 9 8 7 6 5 4 3 2

For sidemen
and their families

Author's Note

I avoided writing *Side Man* for twenty years. This was probably for the best, because during my years as a writer-for-hire, I gained a little perspective and shed a little anger.

After all the rehearsals and performances, I've learned a few things about the playing of the play. Gene, the father, exists in sort of a bubble. When the conversation isn't about music, he's elsewhere; even if he's talking to you. Actors who are used to engaging will find this frustrating. Actors who play Clifford will also be frustrated because he too is a bit of a sideman. If anyone asks, Clifford is always "fine." He does not want to show us everything he is feeling, nor is he even aware of it for most of the play. He feels the same responsibility to the audience that he did to his parents—he keeps things *up* as much as possible, for as long as he can.

If the sidemen keep their emotions in check, Terry, the mother, kind of airs hers out. But the actress playing her should not embrace her craziness. Instead, fight for Terry and for her side of the story. Also, no matter how angry she gets, Terry cares deeply for her husband and especially her son.

The other sidemen, and Patsy, also come with a lot of mileage. I think of Jonesy as looking out for Terry; Patsy as Clifford's guardian; and Al and Ziggy as Gene's section-mates. On stage at least, they cover him. Even though no one actually manages to stop the family's slide, they all do as much as they can. As did all the real-life sidemen and family members on whom these characters are based.

Finally, if you get the chance, listen to the music of this world; to the trumpet kings: Clifford Brown, Fats Navarro, Red Rodney, Lee Morgan, Dizzy, Miles, Chet; and to the sidemen who played, night after night, with Claude Thornhill, Charlie Barnett, Buddy Rich, and Woody Herman.

Special Thanks

When I finally began to write *Side Man* I received generous, unconditional support and insight from a number of actors, directors, musicians, writers, designers, stage crew, and producers. I also received guidance and love from dozens of friends and strangers who have gone through personal dramas like the family in this play. It's been humbling.

I am completely indebted to Michael Mayer for his long devotion to *Side Man*. For his gentle guidance ("this scene is heinous"). For his feel for this world, and for how to make it come to life on stage. Of course, he and I were lucky. We've had good homes: the West Bank, Powerhouse, CSC, and the Roundabout. In addition to the generous actors and designers listed on the following pages, I was helped by: Jeff Binder, Patrick Breen, Nicole Burdette, Geoffrey Cantor, Suzanne Dottino, Tim Guinee, David Henderson, Don Holder, Felicity Huffman, Brian Keane, Bill Lang, Marissa Matrone, Dan Moran, Geoffrey Nauffts, Jack O'Connor, Austin Pendleton, Neil Pepe, and Roger Raines.

Thanks also to a number of the show's Guardian Angels: Peter Manning, who knowingly guided the play on its long journey from Poughkeepsie to Broadway; Jay Harris and the Weissberger Group, who stepped forward early and often. More thanks to: Robbie Baitz, Len Berkmann, Andre Bishop, Eric Bogosian, Jo Bonney, Susann Brinkley, Anne Brooks, Jim Carnahan, Susan Chicoine, Stephanie Coen, Lee Cohen, Burt Collins, Erin Dunn, Beth Emelson, Peter Flaxman, Jenny Gersten, William Goldman, Todd Haimes, Holly Harper, Beth Henley, Drew Hodges, Ron Kastner, Rob Kaufelt, William Kennedy, Mimi Kramer, George Lane, Nile Lanning, Don, Edward, Jody, and Timmy Leight, Local 802, Evan Lurie, Mary Meagher, Peter Marks, Max Mayer, John McCormack, NYSF, Johnny Olson, Daryl Roth, Rudd Simmons, SPOTCO., Gary Springer, and Ron Taft.

Finally, special thanks to Eric Price and Morgan Entrekin who somehow think it still makes sense to publish plays.

Side Man Chronology

Side Man was written while Warren was a member of the New York Playwright's Lab. It was workshopped by Naked Angels in the basement of the West Bank Cafe (February 1996) and was originally produced in June 1996 by New York Stage and Film at Vassar's Powerhouse Theatre.

After its New York City premiere, *Side Man* was nominated for the John Gassner Playwriting Award and several Outer Circle and Drama Desk Awards, including Best Play. Warren won *Newsday*'s Oppenheimer Award given to the Best New American Playwright, and the George and Elisabeth Marton Playwriting Award in the fall of 1998.

THE CAST

(*In order of appearance*)

Clifford	Robert Sella
Terry	Edie Falco
Patsy	Angelica Torn
Gene	Frank Wood
Al	Joseph Lyle Taylor
Ziggy	Michael Mastro
Jonesy	Kevin Geer

Warren Leight's *Side Man* was first produced in New York City at the CSC Theater on March 11, 1998. It was produced by The Weissberger Theater Group (Jay Harris, Producer) and Peter Manning. It was directed by Michael Mayer. The set designs were by Neil Patel, the costume designs were by Tom Broecker, hair and wigs by Bobby H. Grayson, the lighting design was by Kenneth Posner, and the sound design was by Raymond D. Schilke. The production stage manager was Andrea J. Testani.

Side Man premiered on Broadway as the first new play to be produced at the Roundabout Theatre Company's Main Stage on June 25, 1998. Todd Haimes was artistic director and Jay Adler was production supervisor. Wendy Makkena replaced Edie Falco in the role of Terry.

On November 8, 1998, *Side Man* reopened at the John Golden Theatre with new coproducers Ron Kastner, James Cushing, and Joan Stein and general manager Roy Gabay. Christian Slater replaced Robert Sella in the role of Clifford.

Characters

Clifford

Terry

Patsy

Gene

Al

Ziggy

Jonesy

Time: 1985 to 1953
Place: New York City

Act I

Downstage center, lights up on the slightly awkward, twenty-nine-year-old CLIFFORD. To his right, an old bar. Downstage left, a circular booth and table. Clifford faces the audience:

Clifford It's almost . . . (*looks at watch*) oh, I'm late. I'm sure it has nothing to do with the fact that I'm seeing my parents tonight.

Both of them: mom *and* dad; a kind of *This Is Your Life* bender.

I'm not seeing them together, mind you. *Not* a good idea. Definitely not a good idea. Once, long ago, this trumpet player, who I'll probably also see tonight, told me: "The rocksh in her head fit the wholesh in hish."

Not anymore. They haven't seen each other, and I haven't seen him in—

So, OK, it's complicated.

Plus, if I see past all the . . . history, I sense, and this one really screws me up, that things would have been better for them if they'd never had me. But, they did. I'm on the scene, as my old man would say. And even though there are no clean breaks, I swear, tomorrow morning I'm out. So tonight, before the "big reunion" with my father, I have a farewell dinner at Mom's, in the zip code of my youth . . .

Lights up on Clifford's mom, TERRY. She stands in the doorway to her offstage bedroom, smoking a cigarette, alone.

Terry Don't start with me, Clifford—I'm not going over there.

Clifford Ma—I wasn't asking you to—

Terry I can't stand to hear him play—

Clifford I just wanted you to know I was—

Terry I already knew. I had a dream you saw him. And you know what pissed me off? He hasn't aged. He'll never age—nothing gets to him—

Clifford Well, I—

Terry Don't stick up for him, Clifford. You know he gaslit me. Everyone thinks your father's so sweet: "Poor Gene, clean Gene, sweet Gene. How he suffers with crazy Terry."

Clifford No one says—

Terry That rat-bastard gaslit me. (*quick shift, concerned now*) How does he look? *Is he eating?*

Clifford What?

Terry Your father. In the dream. He looked thin.

Clifford How should I know? I haven't seen him.

Terry I made lasagne; there's some containers in the freezer. He can't even feed himself. Will you be home for Christmas?

Clifford I don't know.

Terry You better get going, have a good time . . . There's a box in the hallway with some old photos and magazines. I thought you could use them for your art projects.

Clifford Thanks, Ma.

Terry And tomorrow, on the plane—

Clifford I know Ma: "Say hello to the pilot" when I board.

Terry It keeps them alert if they meet the passengers. Responsible.

Clifford I know, Ma.

She snuffs out her cigarette, as the lights go out on her. Clifford now walks into the Melody Lounge. From an unseen bandstand, a trumpet player solos on "I Remember Clifford."

Clifford I walk in and I hear him before I see him. Playing a ballad. You could play me a hundred trumpet solos and I'd know which one was his. My father's voice.

Listens a bit, fights getting overwhelmed by the music. Goes over to a seat at the bar. Clifford takes it in:

When I was a kid, I thought the Melody Lounge was the coolest place on Earth. In high school, where I was a complete loser, the only thing I had going for me was bringing the guys here to see my old man play trumpet. I was drinking screwdrivers at the bar from the time I was thirteen.

They sound good tonight. All of them. Up there, on the bandstand, a little over two hundred years of musical experience. Ziggy and my dad and Al and Jonesy keep time so well that it's kind of stood still for them, at least when they're playing. They were all horn players in the legendary, completely forgotten Claude Thornhill big band. They recorded things on wire in the forties, right after the war, that are still too hip for the room. (*looks around*) Not that there's anyone in the room tonight. In the audience there's me, two drunks from Jersey, and (*turns to see*) . . . Patsy?

PATSY has walked past the bar and now sees Clifford. She is in her late fifties, but you'd never know it. In her heyday, she stopped traffic on 52nd Street. She hugs him as:

Patsy Clifford? Is that you? I haven't seen you in . . . forever. Does your father know you're here?

Clifford It's kind of a surprise.

Patsy (*looks him over*) You haven't changed—

Clifford Don't tell my shrink—she'd be heartbroken.

Patsy No, you haven't—when you were six, you looked thirty, and you still look thirty . . . So, how's work?

Clifford I quit.

Patsy Good for you.

Clifford I'm going west.

Patsy You *have* changed.

Clifford (*changing the subject*) You haven't. You look great.

Patsy What can I say, it's my cross to bear . . . How's Terry?

Clifford I just came from there—

Lights up on Terry. Music out. She stands in the doorway to her offstage bedroom, smoking a cigarette, alone.

Terry Clifford, what's the name of that Tiny Kahn tune?

Clifford (*to audience*) She does this to me all the time, even when she's not here, she's here. (*to Terry*) "Just My Fucking Luck"?

Terry No, not Kahn, the other one—

Clifford Kern? "Why Was I Born"?

Terry (*she nods*) Yes.

Clifford (*turns to audience*) You kind of have to work with her.

Terry Ask your father to play it.

She closes the door, as lights go out on her. Music up again: "I Remember Clifford."

Clifford OK Ma, "Why Was I Born"? I'll ask.

Patsy Yoo hoo, Clifford.

Clifford (*Returning his attention to Patsy*) Sorry.

Patsy How is she?

Clifford Terry? Good days . . . bad days.

She doesn't push him.

Patsy Old days. You know, (*looks across the stage to the empty booth*) they had their first date here.

Clifford Their only date, I think.

Patsy Once upon a time Clifford, we were in our prime . . . (*she hugs him*) It's been too long.

Clifford (*to audience, during the hug*) Years, actually. Time flies when it crawls. (*to Patsy*) These guys together . . . I can't even think of the last time that happened.

Terry reopens her door. Music out. Patsy retreats upstage.

Terry Well, you know it wasn't on a family vacation or at a restaurant. Or a party. Your father never took us anywhere.

Clifford Ma, please—

Terry All of them—if they're not on a club date, their idea of a big get-together is when they sign for their unemployment check.

Terry closes her door.

Clifford (*to audience*) She can be a little . . . dark. But she's usually right. The last time I saw these guys together was at Unemployment. Nine years ago, at the old 92nd Street Office. The musicians called it Club 92.

Harsh lights up on: Club 92. Clifford stands, walks over to the head of the beginner's unemployment line. Two lines away, his father, GENE, and AL, ZIGGY, and JONESY wait on the old-timer's line.

Clifford (*to audience*) I am twenty-one years old, out of college, out of work. On line for my first unemployment check. It is 1977. As I inch my way up the beginner's line, I spot my father, who is over there (*points*) to sign for what, his four millionth check. As a jazz musician, he is sort of always there. There's the National Endowment for the Arts, which is money for classical musicians, and there's the New York State Bureau of Unemployment, which gives grants to jazz musicians. It's a two-tiered system.

Gene (*calling out to the other musicians*) Al, Ziggy, Jonesy— get a load of this: My kid is signing for his first check.

The guys all see Clifford, shout hellos and wave.

Clifford He is, at that moment, prouder of me than I have ever seen him: Today, I am a man.

Clifford joins Gene, Al, Ziggy and Jonesy in a booth at the Melody Lounge.

Clifford (*to audience*) To celebrate, the old man takes me out afterwards. The guys are in a booth at the back. You can always spot them: they wear car coats, caps, a lot of brown and tan polyester; and they sit as far away from daylight as possible.

Gene (*pointing to Clifford*) My son my son. (*to the guys*) Did you see him?

Handshakes of congratulation.

Al Mazel tov.

Ziggy Geshundheit.

Al Thank you.

Clifford, beaming, now turns back to audience.

Clifford It's a special day. And it will prove to be the only time in my life I'll see my father pick up the check: Not that

Al, Ziggy, or Jonesy picks up a check either. Musicians don't pick up checks. They don't dance. They don't buy when they can rent. They don't care about clothes, shoes, or light. Or weather, except in terms of how it might effect alternate side of the street parking. They order soup:

The waitress comes. It's Patsy. Eight years younger.

Al I'll have the . . . soup.

Ziggy Ish there a shpecial shoup?

Jonesy What do you care? Four soups, Patsy.

Patsy exits to get soups.

Jonesy You want one kid? Five—make it five. Or four soups, one shoup, for Ziggy.

Ziggy Shcrew you. Schmuck. (*shouting*) And um, extra crackersh.

Patsy brings the soups and crackers.

Clifford (*to audience*) Soups come. They wait ten mintues for them to cool down; they're horn players, they can't burn their chops. After a while, I become aware that Jonesy, who has one eye and used to play trombone, is staring at me. Or my arms.

Jonesy stares at Clifford's rolled-up shirtsleeves, or more accurately, at the veins in his exposed forearms.

Jonesy Gene, your kid has great rope. Man—

Clifford (*to audience*) What do you say when an ex-junkie compliments your veins? (*to Jonesy*) Thank you.

Jonesy (*to Gene, very sweet*) No, he does. I wouldn't have said it if I didn't mean it. I mean, Christ, by the time I was his age, I'd shot out so many veins I was reduced to shooting between my toes.

Ziggy We're eating. Ish it too much to ashk . . .

Jonesy Or maybe at that time I was still between my fingers.

Ziggy Thank you. That'sh better.

Jonesy Lost my eye in the war.

He pops his glass eye out and shows it to Clifford and the guys.

Ziggy He shpent the war teaching retarded buglersh reveille.

Jonesy The home front was very dangerous.

Al Ask Dicky Smith.

Everyone laughs. Al explains the reference to Clifford:

Al Piano player, poor schmuck, gets his notice. Now Dickie was clean at that time.

Ziggy A Mormon.

Clifford (*to audience*) A Mormon: this means, a little pot, a couple of times a day. Benzedrine inhalers. Booze.

Al *Clean.* But he's pissing in his pants about being called up. There was a very big war going on at the time.

Ziggy Enormoush.

Al And little Dickie—he doesn't want any part of it. So he goes to Jonesy and says, fix me up. (*explaining to Clifford*) He figures, if he's a junkie, he's automatic 4-F.

Clifford Got it—

Jonesy I tried to warn him—kid, I said, it's so good, don't even try it once. (*to Clifford*) Which is actually what someone said to me when I first started. Which of course only made me want to try it all the more. (*for the table*) So I show him the ropes. What I didn't know is, he's also got someone lobbing him bennies—

Ziggy and Al (*singing*) Everytime it rains it rains, bennies from heaven.

Jonesy And he's knocking back about a quart of bourbon a day. Beer chasers. He spends three weeks just about killing himself, *then* they postpone his friggin' physical. Now by this point, he's pretty strung out—

Al He can't stop even if he wants to—

Jonesy Which you never do, by the way.

Ziggy —Sho he'sh mainlining and taking uppersh and drinking and he'sh loshing weight caushe he'sh vomiting sho much.

Al And he's got the shakes. And he hasn't slept in weeks. And finally—

Jonesy They call him in—and he can barely drag his ass up the stairs. He's down to about ninety-five pounds, his eyes are like bulging out of his forehead. He's lost his hair. He's a total friggin' mess—they take one look at him—they say: "Pal, no point in even giving you a physical"—get this:

Jonesy, Ziggy, Al "You're too fuckin' short."

The guys laugh ahead of the punchline, and through it.

Clifford (*to audience*) The musicians love this story.

Ziggy Too short.

The guys break up again.

Ziggy You get it? He wash like five-two. None of ush ever thought about it. Piano. What differensh did it make?

Jonesy They never even noticed he was a junkie. Me though, I wasn't a junkie then so much as an addict—

Al Ah-huh.

Clifford (*to audience*) It's a subtle distinction.

9

Jonesy But these southern bases were so friggin' hot you had to wear short sleeves all the time, so I can't shoot into my arms, so I'm between my fingers, my toes, and then, into my eye—

Ziggy I would argue thish makesh him a junkie, but—

Jonesy So I had to shoot into my eye. Which only worked for a while.

Al And that's how he got the Purple Heart—

Jonesy —and *lifetime* partial disability.

The guys all salaam-bow to him.

Ziggy (*to Clifford*) Even though he'sh already got dishability, he shtill comesh down every week to shign for hish unemployment check. (*half-serious*) That'sh a work ethic.

Jonesy Thank you. I told the sergeant if I had to go home to Ohio—

Clifford (*to audience*) He was from the Bronx—they all were.

Jonesy —with a jaundiced, pus-leaching sore where my eye—

Ziggy Jeshush Chrisht. Can anyone eat with thish?

Al and Jonesy raise their hands.

Gene The eyes have it.

Everyone laughs. Gene winks at Clifford.

Clifford (*to audience*) These are my role models. My authority figures. My—

Jonesy (*to Clifford*) Hey kid. What kind of horn do you play?

Gene (*to Jonesy*) Bite your tongue. (*to Clifford*) Someone has to make a living in the family.

Ziggy I remember when you wanted lesshonsh. Your old lady shaid no shon of hersh would ever do to another woman what he (*points to Gene*) did to her.

Al and Ziggy (*imitating Terry*) "The rat-bastard."

Everyone laughs at this.

Gene He's still my boy. Managed to get twenty weeks on the books—as a painter.

Al Houses?

Clifford Collages. School job. I cut and paste these—

Gene The kid got a scholarship to some painting school.

Clifford (*to audience*) RISD. Grad school . . .

Gene But instead, he's gonna write for TV. (*to Clifford*) Right?

Ziggy (*impressed*) TV? That'sh a pretty good field. Your father and I were going to do that once.

Clifford I know, I know. But it's not TV—it's advertising. Maybe. I'm up for something.

Ziggy TV paysh pretty good.

Clifford If I get it, yeah. Like twelve hundred a week. But it's not—(*to audience*) The money stops the group cold.

Gene You cop that kind of bread—you work three weeks, you can lay out the whole year.

Everyone agrees.

Clifford (*to audience*) You're listening to jazzonomics. The theory that—

Gene You keep your nut small, you pay your dues, you get to blow your horn.

Al Wait, wait, wait . . . Twelve hundred a *week*? You mean a month, right?

Gene As long as you got a place to flop, the rest is . . . (*he spaces out*)

Clifford (*to audience*) There is no rest. From the time I was four, I knew the family was headed for financial ruin.

Jonesy You gonna finish your crackers?

Jonesy pockets a few cracker packets.

Clifford From the time I was six, I, and everyone else, knew it would be up to me to save us.

Gene I heard about people making money with money, but I always figured that was a sick head to get into—

Clifford (*to audience*) Jazzonomics is why I can't afford to take the RISD scholarship: "Someone has to make a—".

Ziggy (*to Gene—figuring out "the catch"*) Yeah, yeah, but how doesh he collect next year if he jusht worksh three weeksh?

Gene Here's the beauty part. I already got my twenty weeks in. So every week *I'm* on the books now, I lose a check.

Clifford (*to audience*) This kind of talk used to drive my mother crazy.

Gene So the *kid* works three weeks at his TV gig. Quits. Then I do club dates under *his* name, the union won't know—

Al —you work seventeen weeks under his name,—

Ziggy —*he* getsh hish twenty weeksh in—

Jonesy —that way *you* collect—

Al (*to Clifford*) —he pays you cash for the gigs you do in his name—

Gene (*to Clifford*) You're getting your weeks, I'm—

Clifford Dad, Dad—It's not TV, it's advertising. I don't have the job yet. I may not get it. And if I do get the gig, I may not quit. (*group is appalled*) I mean, it might be worth trying to stay.

Gene (*to the guys, winking*) I have no son.

The guys crack up. Patsy returns, with five separate checks.

Patsy Here you go fellas.

Gene signals for her to give him all the checks. The men, and Patsy, stop in mid-breath.

Gene No, no, my treat. (*to Patsy*) My boy signed for his first check today.

Patsy Did you really? Congratulations, Gene!

Clifford nonchalantly shrugs. Gene beams.

Patsy Drop by later kid, I'll buy you a drink.

Al, Ziggy, Jonesy ogle Patsy as she walks away.

Patsy Keep it in your pants, boys.

Gene stares at his son.

Clifford (*to audience*) My father covers the checks, and then, he does something else he's almost never done. He looks at me. He just stops and stares. And I think he sees something, some promise, some sadness, or . . .

Gene starts to whistle the first phrase of "The Afternoon of a Faun."

Clifford waves a hand in front of his father's face: no reaction.

Clifford He's gone now. Back to when he had no son, back to 1953—before the Beatles, before Elvis. When these guys were like ballplayers. On the road, written up in the papers, endorsing trumpets in *Down Beat*. Bands passing each other in the night even traded sidemen: one first trumpet player and an alto for a second trumpet and a tenor to be named later.

Lights fade on the guys as they exit, and come up on a dimly lit hotel basement—overhead pipes, low ceiling, white walls. Clifford sets up a few folding chairs.

NOTE: Throughout the rest of the first act Clifford, when narrating, also stage manages, or plays caretaker to his parents and their friends. He hands or receives props, drinks, instruments, clothes, and even does simple set changes. He is engaged and in motion throughout.

Clifford It was after such a trade my father found himself returning to New York, to his usual room—nine dollars a week—at the Hotel Nevada, an old Upper West Side dive. Mom told me that after road trips, he'd stay there a couple of weeks, until he was clean enough to go home to his mother in the Bronx. The Nevada let the musicians practice in the basement . . . Right now, a young flutist thinks she has the place all to herself.

Lights up on Terry—Clifford hands a flute to a young Terry as she enters. She is 24, fresh-scrubbed face, curly Italian hair. Hand-sewn clothes. She starts to play "The Afternoon of a Faun." Sweet, simple tone. She misses a note.

Terry Fuck.

Terry takes a breath, starts to play again. She gets to the same passage. Hits the same clam: DAAAH-DUH-DAH DUH DAA DAH. She cannot find the right note.

Terry Fuck.

Now from somewhere else amidst the pipes, a sweet trumpet starts the phrase again, in the flutist's key, echoing her and correcting her at the same time. Gets to the area where she's wiped out, slows down, gracefully plays through the phrase: Da-duh deee-dah. She listens. Then picks up her flute, starts again.

In unison now, slowly: Da-duh deee-dah. They play together for a while, he now starts to swing the melody. She gets to another tricky spot, wipes out. This time he quotes her wipe out, riffs on it. Starts to really improvise on the phrase.

Terry Fuck.

She puts her flute down. Starts to disassemble it and put it in her case. He continues to improvise on Debussy. His sound gets jazzier.

Terry (*to herself*) Showoff.

Clifford stands at the bar unseen by Gene or Terry. Now Gene enters.

Gene Name that tune.

She looks up.

Terry Mine or yours?

Gene Yours.

Terry How many seconds?

Gene (*whistles the tune again*) As many as you want, just name it.

Terry What do I win?

Gene (*thinking*) A ticket to see Woody Herman?

Terry How can you get a ticket?

Gene Friends of mine are in the band.

Terry You're teasing me.

Gene You have six seconds. Five . . . Four . . . Three . . . t—

Terry Time out. Stop the clock. You don't know it?

Gene It doesn't swing.

Terry It did when you played it.

Gene Are you new in town?

Terry I've been here four days, thank you.

Gene My mistake. It's classical, right? (*whistles first few notes again*) My mother played it when I was—

Terry Your mother played trumpet?

Gene No. Cello. With Casals.

Terry Pablo?

Gene Him too.

Terry And you don't know it?

Gene Only had two lessons. She caught me roller-skating with her cello. Made me study trumpet, with her father.

Terry A jazz trumpet player?

Gene Moscow Symphony. Tell me what it is. *Please* . . . I'll never be able to nap unless I get it out of my head.

Terry "Afternoon of a Faun." Debussy. (*Mispronounced: De-BOO-sy*)

    Gene is greatly relieved.

Terry Whatever the fuck a faun is.

Gene It's a little deer.

Terry Ohh.

Gene . . . dear. Useful for crosswords.

Terry (*very impressed*) You do crosswords?

Gene Sure.

Terry Shit.

Gene You know all the other four-letter words. I'm surpised you don't know fawn.

Terry Screw you . . .

Terry starts to walk away.

Gene Cold front. Feel the breeze. Catch you later.

Clifford goes to her.

Clifford Ma—that's not how this ends . . .

Terry (*to Clifford*) It would have been a lot easier—

Clifford Yeah, but . . .

Terry (*to Clifford*) All right.

Clifford takes her flute, hands her a wrapped sandwich. Then she and Gene replay the scene from a second before:

Terry Screw you . . .

Terry starts to leave again, but—

Terry . . . dear.

Gene turns to her. Smiles.

Gene It's Genie.

Terry "Genie?" Make a wish?

Gene Genie Glimmer. Gene.

He puts out his cuff-linked, manicured hand for her to shake.

Terry Anna Maria Prencipe Defeceo Abbruzese.

Gene What do they call you for short?

Terry Crazy Terry.

Gene Sure. Why not—

Terry My brother Guy says I look like St. Teresa when she was hallucinating.

Gene She wasn't hallucinating, the chick was having a major orgas—

Terry You look like you're starving. Do you want some of this?

She offers him her sandwich. Gene shakes his head.

Gene I'm fine.

Terry (*maternal*) You don't have to be embarrassed 'cause your hungry. I mean, I don't have a pot to piss in, or a window to throw it out. But you shouldn't go without eating. Here, have some.

Gene takes a huge bite out of the sandwich.

Terry When was the last time you had something to eat?

Gene (*chewing, shameless*) An hour ago. Bickfords. Breakfast.

Terry Breakfast? It's three in the afternoon.

Gene I just got back into town at six this morning—Woody's band.

Terry You're in Woody's . . .

Gene We're in Philly, we play 'til four, then onto the bus with my road tour pillow. (*He double-joints his arms over his head*) Now I'm trying to get some life back into my chops before tonight.

Terry What's tonight?

Gene The Paramount. Thanks for the sandwich.

Terry *The* Paramount?

Gene As far as I know.

Gene nods, it's no big deal to him, it's unthinkably glamorous to her.

Terry You can't *really* get me a ticket?

Gene It'll be at the door, kid.

Gene takes the sandwich, walks off. Terry turns to Clifford who brings her a coat and purse. Slowly, we start to hear the sound of a big swing band.

Terry (*to Clifford*) I went.

Clifford He really got you a ticket?

Terry *He* couldn't get a ticket, so he met me at the stage door. He told me to stay in the basement—

Clifford Classy—

Terry —but I snuck upstairs and watched from the wings.

We listen with Terry to the sound of a soaring trumpet section. Soloing above them now, a heartbreakingly beautiful trumpet.

Terry (*to Clifford*) He has a beautiful tone. I went to the band room afterwards to tell him.

Ziggy, Al, Jonesy, all younger, zoot-suited, packing up. They are in their prime. A lot of bustle except for Gene who seems to move in his own incredibly slow world. Ziggy watches him.

Jonesy Nice blowing Genie.

Gene Not me, it was Ziggy's charts—

Ziggy They shound like shit until *you* sholo.

Gene I really couldn't get anything going up there. My chops are hanging . . .

They all look at him.

Clifford (*to audience*) He stole the show, and he has no idea.

Terry (*to Clifford*) He never had any idea.

Ziggy Hey turtle, shcrew you. We'll be over at Charlie'sh.

The guys start to leave. Al, always on the prowl, notices Terry.

Al (*to Terry*) Hey orphan, you want to come?

Terry (*goes to Gene*) I'm with him.

Gene (*noticing her for the first time*) You're still here?

Terry (*confessing*) I snuck upstairs, and heard you, you sounded so—

Al (*to Terry, on his way out*) Beautiful doll, if he's still packing up in half an hour, c'mon over on your own.

Jonesy (*to Al*) Let's go Romeo, libation awaits.

Al (*to Terry*) Ask for table 69.

This breaks the guys up. Terry doesn't get it.

Ziggy (*about Al and Gene*) One man'sh an octopush, the other'sh a turtle.

They leave. Terry and Gene alone now in the band room. Clifford hands Gene his trumpet case.

Terry Are you the turtle?

Gene (*proud*) They did a contest, on the road, Krupa's band. They timed all the slow guys. How we ate, how long it took us to pack up, to shave. I had no idea this was going on. Some of the guys knew, were *trying* to go slow. But I still beat everybody.

She starts to help him pack. Touches the horn to put it in the case. He swiftly takes the horn away from her.

Gene Hey—don't touch the horn! Never touch the horn.

He lays it in the case, as if it were glass.

Terry You sounded beautiful out there.

Gene That guy Al, Romeo we call him, best lead player in town. Can sight-read fly shit at 500 feet.

Terry But you're the one who gets to solo. You know who you sound like? (*she puffs her cheeks out*) You sound like Dizzy.

Gene (*he covers her mouth*) Don't ever say that in front of the guys.

Terry There's something you do that he does.

Gene Just an octave and a half lower.

Terry You don't know how good you are. You know that?

Gene You want to go over to Charlie's? (*she nods*) Good. Just do not mention me and Dizzy in the same sentence. I am not worthy.

Clifford watches as Terry and Gene walk out.

Clifford They go across the street to Charlie's Melody Lounge. Where we are now: same tablecloths, same songs on the jukebox, same smell.

They cross over to the Melody: neon-lit, red-checked hamburger joint. There's a big round booth in the back; Al and Ziggy are already there.

Clifford Ziggy has already bought the next morning's papers—he's obsessed with Joe McCarthy.

Ziggy (*looking up from his paper*) Anti-shemitic bashtard.

Terry and Gene walk to the booth. He signals the guys.

Gene Boys, this is Terry. Terry, I'd like to introduce the trumpet section.

Ziggy and Al now rise and do shtick:

Al (*to Ziggy*) I'm Al.

Ziggy (*to Al*) I'm Ziggy.

Al and Ziggy (*to each other*) How do you do?

They shake each others' hands, then they sit back down. Patsy now arrives with drinks.

Patsy (*to Terry*) And I'm Patsy, Romeo's piece on the side.

Ziggy (*pointing to Al's toupée*) Not to be confewshed with hish piece on top.

Everyone makes a face at this. Ziggy shrugs.

Patsy What are you drinking?

Terry Water's OK.

Patsy Water? Genie, another one out for your money. What do you do, meet these girls the moment they step off the boat?

Ziggy Order a drink, honey, itsh polite. (*about Patsy*) She'sh putting hershelf through medical shchool. One intern at a time.

Terry (*has no idea what's going on*) I'll have a . . .

Patsy and Terry Shirley Temple.

Patsy goes offstage as Jonesy now lurches into the booth.

Ziggy Incoming!

Jonesy has evidently shot up, Terry is worried by his state, the others take it completely in stride. He passes out, slowly, face flat on the table.

Ziggy (*makes an umpire's call*) Shafe!

Terry Is he OK?

Gene Honey, he's fine. He just likes to . . . relax after a gig.

Terry is oblivious to the cause of his condition, but she is concerned.

Terry He doesn't look so good.

Ziggy He doeshn't feel sho bad—

Terry (*in Jonesy's ear*) What did you eat today? Did you have tuna? I bet you had tuna, mayonnaise—you have to be very careful in warm weather.

She lifts Jonesy's head off the table. Al and Ziggy are laughing. She takes a napkin, dips it in water, wipes his brow.

Terry (*to Jonesy, loud*) Was it tuna? Does anything hurt?

Jonesy (*nods back in for a second*) Jesus, Gene, you didn't tell me you were dating Florence Nightingale.

He nods back out.

Over to the bar, where Patsy, dressed in the coat she wore at the beginning of the play, enters and resumes her 1985 talk with Clifford. Music goes back to "I Remember Clifford" last heard when Clifford entered the Melody Lounge.

Patsy How's Terry?

Clifford Good days, bad days—

Patsy Old days. She was something else back then, Clifford.

Patsy and Clifford look across the stage to the booth: they watch Terry take the lit cigarette out of Jonesy's hand and put it out. He doesn't notice.

Clifford (*to Patsy*) She still has her moments: just got kicked out of her senior center crafts course for crocheting obscene homilies.

Patsy I tried calling, but she—

Clifford She doesn't talk to too many people.

Patsy Everyone always turns on Terry. You know your father and I never—

Clifford Even if you did, he wouldn't have noticed.

Patsy Don't be mean, you. (*listens to the music*) He's playing "I Remember Clifford."

Clifford Genie on a ballad—break your heart every time.

She kisses him on the cheek—music out, lights cross fade as Clifford helps Patsy take off her coat. She leaves him and crosses the stage, over to the booth, drinks in hand. It's 1953 again.

Patsy I'm off for a while.

She sits on Al's lap, while he finishes rolling a joint.

Gene So's Jonesy.

Terry I think he may have had some bad tuna. He doesn't look very good.

Patsy Wait a few minutes . . .

Ziggy He'll look worshe.

While they've been talking, Al and the guys have started passing the joint. He passes it to Patsy.

Terry You roll your own? I should do that. It's much more economical.

Patsy (*to Gene, while taking a hit off the joint*) Is she for real?

The joint is passed from Al, to Ziggy, to Gene, to Terry, who, thinking it's a cigarette, takes a drag. Keeps up her nervous monologue.

Terry I don't smoke that much. The only reason I started smoking at all was because the sisters at St. Mary's accused me of smoking all the time, so I finally figured I'd start smoking—Pall Mall Golds, 'cause that's what my brother Guy, he's a narcotics agent,

Ziggy, Al, Gene, and even Jonesy cough on this. Terry doesn't miss a beat:

Terry . . . smoked; although nobody ever accused him of smoking. And I've seen people roll their own in the movies, but aren't you clever for rolling your own like this. And then, the way you all share—(*hands the joint to Gene*) Here . . .

Patsy What planet did you come from?

Terry Baltimore. Not originally. East Boston originally, but I can't go back because my husband, Dominic Defeces, the bricklaying prick, just left me, in Baltimore. I wrote Blimpie, she's my oldest sister, there's seven others, that I had to come home, and she wrote me and told me: "Don't come back." 'Cause my mother, Italian, Catholic, thinks divorce is a sin— even though the rat-bastard got an annulment to run off with my best friend, she'll make me join a fuckin' convent in Montana, if I do. Go home. So Blimpie, Cupie, Fat Raffie, and some of my other sisters pitched in and sent me a money tree with twenty-five dollars. So I came to New York. The room's eight, so now I'm down to thirteen dollars, but I can't go home. But I'm not worried because—

Ziggy Anybody following thish?

Jonesy (*looks up from his haze*) I am.

Al What's she saying?

Jonesy Her prick husband, a mudslinger, took her from East Boston, which is a fuckin' tough ghetto, let me tell you, and left her in Baltimore. But Italians don't divorce—so she had to come here. Good-night now. (*He nods back out*)

Ziggy You're in luck then. Jazz musiciansh divorce all the time. Patshy's on her third trumpet player.

Terry You and Al are married?

Patsy No. I mean, I am, he's not. My husband's on the road.

Ziggy Romeo'sh what you call the relief band. Shpeaking of which, we're due downtown in o . . . (*looks at watch*) twenty minutesh ago.

Patsy And I'm back in . . .

Al We'll hop a cab, (*to Ziggy*) your treat.

Ziggy (*grabbing Jonesy off the table*) I'll have to roll Joneshy. Genie, you coming?

Gene I'll catch up with you later.

Terry (*as the gang leaves*) Nice to meet you all. (*to Gene*) It's amazing how economical you all are.

> *Terry holds the remains of the joint, but since it's now roach size, and since she thinks it's a cigarette, she just puts it out in an ashtray.*

Terry It's pretty much down to the end. Here, have one of mine.

> *Gene watches in shock. Now Gene takes Terry's hand and leads her out of the bar, and across the stage.*

Clifford They didn't make it downtown that night, instead he took her to his room in the Hotel Nevada, for a nightcap. That's when she saw:

> *Lights up on a bare room, as Terry and Gene enter.*

Terry (*to Gene, now in his room*) You have a sink?

Gene State of the art: Cold comes out of the hot, cold comes out of the cold—

Terry looks at the photos on the wall.

Terry Is that you with Frank Sinatra?

Gene When he comes to town, he usually adds me to his—

Terry Oh my God, I've wanted to see him my whole life. More than anything.

Gene Next time he's here, I'll get you in.

Clifford hands him a wire-recorder. Gene fiddles with it.

Terry Wait a minute, you're bullshitting me. Right? Everyone always does that. You didn't really play with him, did—

Gene Here, this is me with him at the Copa—recorded it from backstage on this very wire recorder.

A choppy quality, but recognizable Sinatra bootleg, live from the Copa. A trumpet section soars behind Sinatra.

They listen for a few bars.

Terry That's so beautiful.

Gene The club manager caught me with it, picked up the whole wire recorder, threw it against the wall. It still plays. We were gonna write to the company, see if they'd do an endorsement ad. "Famed Copa Manager and Hoodlum Jules Podell Couldn't Break This, Neither Will You."

They listen for a few moments. Terry goes to Gene. She grabs his hand.

Terry Do you want to dance? With me?

Gene Trumpet players don't dance—bad for the chops. Come here, let's just listen.

He takes her in his arms. They kiss, as the voice of Sinatra comes up, and the lights fade down.

27

Clifford That night, with the help of Frank Sinatra, they made love. Then slept together, very close, in a single bed with the blinking neon of the Hotel Nevada flickering off and on.

He watches them sleep as the lights fade up.

Clifford Morning comes, and Terry's a little more chipper than he is.

Terry (*to Gene*) Do you want to live together?

He jumps.

Gene I'm going on the road in a couple of weeks. Maybe sooner.

Terry I'll find us a place while you're gone. When you come back, it will be all fixed up.

Gene No—it's out of the—

Terry moves into their new apartment. Gene, in shock, tries to move quickly after her. But even when he moves quickly he's slow. The doorbell rings.

Terry We're in here!

Ziggy, Al, and Jonesy arrive with furniture, from busted marriages, for the next scene; Gene remains in the last scene, or a limbo, for a little while.

Ziggy (*with Al, carrying a couch*) The Sheven Shantini are here, minush four.

Al Where do you want this?

Jonesy unrolls a rug onto the floor.

Ziggy We were going to let Al carry the rug, but he already hash one.

Terry supervises as Gene exits.

And, like that—they're moved in. Terry shows Al, Ziggy, and Jonesy where everything goes; she rearranges things.

Al Hey, Terry. Nice crib.

Terry There's a crib coming?

Jonesy Four-letter word baby.

Terry (*getting it*) Ohhh.

Ziggy (*struggling to find something to compliment*) The floorsh look good.

Jonesy walks in with a lamp. Al plugs it in, as Terry embarks on another monologue.

Terry I did them by hand. I fucked-up my fingers something awful. Then I made the curtains out of some tablecloths I stole from Charlie's. You know those nice red and white ones, I went in, had a coffee, and I started pulling the thing off the table. Patsy looks at me, and says, "What are you doing?" So I says to her, "I'm stealing a tablecloth to make curtains, what does it look like?" She came back with three more tablecloths in a paper bag, "Here," she says, "the new manager is a prick."

Al and Ziggy have no idea what she's talking about. Jonesy followed her perfectly. She exits to kitchen. The guys are alone.

Al (*sotto voce*) So dig this guys—It's four a.m., I'm in my bed, there's a knock at the door. I open it, there's this beautiful blond in a full-length mink coat. She says, "Are you Al Paradisio?" I say, "Baby, I'm anyone you want me to be." She pops open da mink—nuttin' on—"Happy Birthday," she says, "From Charlie Barnett."

Ziggy Cockshucker gave me cuff linksh.

Now Gene walks in cradling an oversized nondescript box that he seems to believe is very delicate.

Gene Hey guys, check it out.

Al Whoa. Easy does it, let it down nice and easy.

Gene I copped it from Leon.

Terry (*entering*) What is that thing?

Gene It's an orgone box.

Terry Orgone? Like the Japanese POWs used to do? After the war I worked at a holding camp and—

Ziggy What ish she talking about—

Jonesy (*gently explaining*) That's origami, this is orgone.

Ziggy How come he undershtandsh her?

Gene Orgone box—Wilhelm Reich designed it.

Al (*to Gene*) Does she know about Reich?

Terry What did he play?

This cracks Ziggy and Jonesy up. Now Al lights a joint.

NOTE: *They are all pretty close to high to begin with, so they get stoned quickly. On the other hand, they're pretty used to being stoned, so it's not like they're seeing colors or anything.*

Gene Wilhelm Reich. Shrink, writes about . . . (*takes the joint, inhales*)

Al . . . about the armor that people carry on themselves.

Al passes the joint to Terry, who still smokes it like a cigarette.

Al . . . it's caused by sexual repression, from the society, the family, and it causes people to develop . . . armor. Which they think protects them—

Jonesy Honey, can you pass that?

She takes one more drag on the joint, coughs.

Terry You guys get the shittiest tobacco.

Al —but, you see, what the armor really does is shut them off from just . . . fucking freely without shame. (*in mid-toke*) Now you see good sex, I'm talking really good sex— (*finishes toke*)

Ziggy Like with shomeone whoshe awake—

The others look at him.

Al —really good sex, releases orgones. Which are this positive energy. And that box collects those orgones.

Gene That's what this box does.

Terry You guys are fucking weird.

Jonesy Put your hand inside.

Terry What?

Ziggy You shaid you hurt your hand, shcraping the floorsh, right? Jusht put your hand inshide.

Terry's not sure what to do.

Gene Go ahead. It's OK.

She does.

Jonesy I can't believe Leon's old lady won't let him keep his box.

Gene His old lady's moving him to Massachusetts.

Ziggy Who'sh he gonna play with in Masha, Mashaschu— fuck it, Boshton.

Al What play? She wants him out of the business.

Jonesy Leon? Neon Leon? Tell me he could get a job other than playing trumpet.

Terry Who's Neon Leon?

Gene Neon Leon. I told you about him. The one Benny Goodman fired because he peed onstage.

Jonesy (*as Leon, stage whispers*) Benny, Benny—I gotta go.

Al (*as Benny Goodman*) That's not my problem, Neon, you knew about this gig weeks ago.

Jonesy (*as Leon*) Benny, what am I supposed to do?

Al (*as Benny*) You can pee on the stage for all I care.

Ziggy Sho he did.

Al He's a motherfucker, though. Let's face it, he's a motherfucker.

The guys all agree, he's a motherfucker.

Jonesy Total motherfucker.

Terry Is motherfucker good or bad?

Jonesy (*gently explaining*) G's above high C, all night long.

Gene What a waste, chops like that, going to law school.

Ziggy We oughtta have a wake: Requiem for a Motherfucker.

Lights dim on them, lights up on Clifford, as a funeral march, Louis Armstrong's "St. James Infirmary," plays.

Clifford (*to audience*) A moment of silence. For Leon. Since he's leaving the business, in effect, he's passed away. Over the years there'd be more and more of these moments. Guys would O.D., or go to jail, or worse get married and have to work 9 to 5. By the time I was on the scene, these guys were sort of an underground railroad to the straight world. We got our eyeglasses from a former tenor player, car insurance from an alto, and of course that box, from Leon.

Back to the living room, music out.

Jonesy How's your hand?

Terry What?

Jonesy Your hand.

She takes it out of the box. Stares at it.

Terry Holy shit. It's better. It's almost healed.

Jonesy HALLELUJAH.

Terry (*scared*) What the fuck is in there?

Ziggy and Al (*spooky-voice*) *Orrrr-gooones.*

Gene Don't ever tell anyone we have one of these things.
They're illegal. They're chasing Reich all over the country.

Terry You guys are fuckin' weird. I don't want that thing in
my house. Get it out.

Gene Calm down, Terry. It's harmless.

Terry I'm serious, get it out.

Ziggy Wait 'til she shee's the resht of Leon's shtuff.

*Terry, very quickly, loses it. She starts to beat Gene's chest
with her hands. He grabs them.*

Terry Don't tease me. I hate when you all do that.

Gene Terry, no one is doing anything to you.

Terry (*embarrassed, calming down*) OK—still, get it out of
the house.

Jonesy (*going to the door*) C'mon guys. Let's—

Al I want to stay and watch.

Ziggy C'mon, Al.

They leave. Gene goes to her, holds her. Calms her down.

Terry Is that thing really illegal?

Gene Nobody knows what it is, so we can't get in trouble.

Terry Do we have to have it in the house?

Gene I'll take care of it.

She calms down.

Patsy enters at the booth of the Melody Lounge. Terry crosses to her.

Patsy So, what's the problem?

Terry Gene's got some box. He says it's illegal. And it collects oregons that—

Patsy Orgones. Leon used to have one.

Terry (*happy this story checks out*) That's where Genie got it.

Patsy Leon's old lady probably made him give it up. She made him give everything else up—which is more than I ever got him to do.

Terry You went out with Neon Leon?

Patsy Neon was my first husband. Not that he'd remember. The Big Junked-Out Lug. I told him, "If you really become a lawyer, I'll let you handle all my divorces."

Terry I couldn't make it through another divorce. When Dominic left me, I thought I'd go crazy.

Patsy They get easier. After a while, it's like falling off a bicycle.

Terry That rat-bastard—left me for my best friend. You and Genie never—

Patsy (*laughs*) Oh, honey. No. Never. I promise.

Terry Leon wasn't really a junkie, was he?

Patsy Doll, you don't have to worry about that with Gene. Gene's clean. He's the one they all call when their cars break down.

Terry nods, without really following this.

Clifford (*to audience*) This was some sort of code, 'cause these guys' cars always break, (*to Terry*) and half of them don't even have cars.

Clifford hands Terry a dinner tray with two soup bowls. She crosses to the living room.

Clifford (*to audience*) It took a while, but Mom started to get the gist of Patsy's field work on trumpet players.

Back to the apartment, a quiet dinner. Terry serves Gene. He eats slowly, blows on his soup.

Terry Patsy says these doo-wop groups don't even use horns.

Gene She's married three trumpet players in a row, so she must think there's some future in it.

Terry She says the big bands are gone for good. And a lot of the clubs are—

Gene Terry, trust me, it's nothing to worry about. I'm a professional. Like a doctor, or a lawyer. And here in New York, with all the TV and radio here. You can't ask for a more secure field—every station will have to have its own band. Honest.

Terry Then why is Patsy's husband getting out?

Gene That's her ex-husband. The second one. Stu. Not Bernie. Bernie's a motherfucker—he's out on the road sixty weeks a year. When he comes back to town, Charlie Barnett's gonna add him to the band, and we'll record.

Terry Then why is Stu getting out?

Gene Stu's a lead player. Great chops, but he can only work the big bands. But I'm a true sideman—I can solo, back up a singer—

Terry Or fake Deboosy

Gene And harmony. Three part. Four part. I'm a . . . a—

Terry A jack-of-all-trades.

Gene Bingo.

They kiss, then she pulls back.

Terry Wait—it wasn't just Stu—Al too. She said he hasn't even had a Saturday night this month.

Gene That won't happen. To me. I mean, look: if there ever comes a Saturday night when I'm not booked, just one Saturday night, then—I promise, I'll get out of the business, OK?

Terry You don't have to say that.

Gene But I can. It's the easiest promise I could ever make.

She kisses him.

Terry Are you going to be on the road a lot?

Gene I used to think I was. But you came in and (*looks around*) . . .

Terry You like it?

Gene I've never had a home in my life—I like it a lot.

Terry Patsy's gonna get me a job waitressing soon, at Charlie's. So you won't have to—

Gene No. I don't want you working. I'm a little behind now—with the car breaking down, and the rent—but we're almost out of the woods. And, (*looks straight into her eyes*) I promise you. I'm going to take care of us, (*kisses her*) you won't ever have to work at all.

Terry stands.

Terry (*yelling to a kitchen's short-order window*) BLT please, whiskey down.

From the other side of the stage now, Patsy, in a waitress uniform, meets Terry downstage, hands her an apron.

Patsy (*to an unseen cook*) Fry two, in butter please, not grease. Thank you. (*to Terry*) The prick at table six is waving for you.

Terry He tries to cop a feel every time I refill his coffee.

Patsy If he does it again, spill some on his lap. How's Genie? (*to cook*) *Can I have my eggs please?*

Terry He's going to record soon with Charlie Barnett. He says after that we should be squared away.

Patsy (*subtle announcement*) Are you gonna come to my wedding?

Terry Patsy, that's great! (*she gives Patsy a big hug, then:*) Who are you marrying?

Patsy *Al.* I've been in love with him since Leon and I were engaged.

Terry Good for you.

Patsy (*to cook*) Where the fuck are my eggs?

Terry Does Al mind you waitressing?

Patsy Somebody has to make a living.

Terry Genie can't stand it. He says—

Patsy He'll get used to it—they all do.

Over to Clifford, at the bar; while he speaks, the guys return to the apartment, with ever more stuff. They place an end table down, upside down, it's bottom shelf now at top.

Ziggy looks at the end table. Something's wrong.

Ziggy (*to Jonesy*) Shomething'sh wrong.

Now they see the problem. Pick it up and clock it 180 degrees, still upside down, however.

Ziggy and Jonesy Aaaahhh.

They go back outside for more stuff.

NOTE: *Throughout the rest of the play, the portion of the stage that is their apartment will go from bare to full to cluttered to cramped: Mismatched furniture, slightly broken or chipped chairs, frayed carpet.*

Clifford While the rest of the country was moving to the suburbs, Mom and Dad stayed in the city. Nine floors up. Rent controlled. Little by little their place filled up. The apartment became "the hangout" before I was born. The lamps were from Ziggy's first marriage.

Ziggy enters with two lamps.

Terry (*to herself*) Sweet kid, what was her name?

She joins Clifford at the bar. Gene sits on the couch, ignoring her.

Ziggy Shushie.

Terry (*to Clifford*) Right. Susie—then he broke up with her, and dated . . . Cecelia?

Ziggy Sheshily.

Ziggy leaves. Terry continues with Clifford:

Terry I told Ziggy: "Date someone whose name you can pronounce. Lana. Diane."

Clifford (*to audience*) When Patsy finally divorced Bernie to marry Al, we . . . they—(I'm not on the scene yet)—got Bernie's stuff.

Patsy and Al come on—lovebirds for the moment. She carries a box of Bernie's records, mariachas, and bongos. Al carries Bernie's hi-fi.

Patsy (*to Terry*) Ziggy's moving in with Sheshily. Get this: Sheventy Shecond Shtreet.

Al (*to the girls*) It'll never last. She's a call girl.

Terry (*doesn't get the problem*) What's wrong with working for an answering service?

Patsy It's doomed—they'll each want the other to get out of the business.

Terry (*to Clifford*) Patsy was right. Ziggy went back on the road. We got his hi-fi.

Gene stays in his own world on the couch. Jonesy comes in, carrying a TV set, placed center stage. Ziggy brings a six-pack of beer.

Patsy and Al neck—for a moment. Then she stops. Slaps him.

Terry Then, six months after they got married, Patsy and Al split up, and we got Al's TV set. And Al for a couple of months—on Bernie's couch.

Jonesy and Ziggy move Al, as if he were another hand-me-down, onto the couch. Patsy plugs in the TV.

Patsy This was almost my TV. Twice.

Terry and Patsy exit.

Gene, Al, Ziggy, and Jonesy sit and watch TV. Ziggy passes out a six-pack, looks at the furnishings.

Ziggy Genie, the Shalvation Army ish ready to talk peace—

Gene (*to the guys*) I tell Terry, our apartment is furnished in Early American Divorce.

The guys break up at this. Terry returns with plates of food. Patsy turns on the hi-fi. A party tableau: Patsy dances with Ziggy. A 1950s conga line starts: Ziggy, Patsy, Gene, Terry, Al—and finally Jonesy—playing bongos at the rear of the line.

In the living room, everyone freezes. A flash goes off: A HAPPY TIMES PHOTO. They are captured on film in one final happy moment.

Clifford (*looks at photos from long ago, looks in the living room at the party*) From what I understand, EVERYONE WAS HAPPY BEFORE I WAS BORN.

Everyone looks at Clifford, then:

Patsy He's on!

The line splits up. All grab seats to watch the TV.

Terry They're only showing him from the waist up. They're scared shitless.

Clifford (*to audience*) This would be the night Elvis first played the Ed Sullivan Show.

Group, this time including Patsy, who's now arm-in-arm with Ziggy, watches Elvis on TV. Jonesy stares intensely at the screen. "Hound Dog" ends to TV cheers, Jonesy turns the set off.

Jonesy Anybody here know how to play guitar?

Gene, Ziggy, Al shake their heads.

Jonesy Too bad. That kid will do to horn players what talkies did to Buster Keaton. Mark my words.

They all look at him. Terry is the only one who doesn't laugh. Al follows Jonesy as he leaves.

Terry (*to Clifford*) Jonesy got arrested that night. Your father told me he got plastered and they took away his cabaret card, for disorderly conduct, which meant he couldn't work in New York, and we got his coffee table.

Al puts the coffee table in front of the couch. Ziggy and Patsy, who are necking on the couch, put their plates down on it without losing a beat, then exit after Al.

Clifford hands Terry a postcard.

Terry He moved to Vegas for the year. Said it was wide open and (*to Gene*) WE SHOULD COME DOWN.

Gene Las Vegas? It's in the middle of a desert.

Terry Jonesy's doing well there, and he plays trombone. I have a feeling that—

Gene You run the kitchen, let me take care of business. Vegas is never gonna—there's no future in it. It's a mirage.

Terry (*while clearing plates and bottles to the kitchen*) What about L.A.? Ziggy says some of the TV shows are moving there.

Gene Terry—it won't happen. New York is where the work is, and always will be.

Clifford (*from the bar*) Gene was sort of an anti-psychic. But Mom was raised to believe papa knew best. And Pops was a City College man, after all. Besides, by now, Gene and Ziggy had gotten the idea that they could make it big as comedy writers for the Sid Ceasar show.

Clifford hands Gene and Ziggy two scripts. They pace back and forth, scripts in hand, working on their comedy routine. Terry watches.

Ziggy (*reading the script, in the voice of a British Queen*) "Damnation, shays the Queen, the Duke goeth down not before I, hish Royal Highnessh?"

Gene (*mock British*) "He giveth no Crown? Wouldst her ladyship prefer him beheaded or . . . hung?"

Ziggy (*reading the Queen*) "You fool, if he'd been hung in the firsht place, he wouldsh't not need hish head at all."

They laugh themselves silly. Then leave. Terry watches them go.

Terry (*to Clifford*) They must have spent a hundred hours on those scripts. But they never sent them out.

Patsy, with two drinks in hand, meets the twenty-one-year-old Clifford, in a booth at Charlie's. It is 1977.

Patsy Here you go, Clifford. In honor of your first unemployment check. Cheers.

Clifford Thanks.

Patsy And these are for you too.

She drops an envelope on the table, stuffed with papers.

Clifford What are they?

Patsy Gene told me you're going to study TV, in Rhode Island. And I remembered, I still had some of his and Ziggy's scripts, I thought maybe you could—

Clifford No, Genie gets it . . . wrong. I got a scholarship for Art School, in Rhode Island.

Patsy Ohh. Well, congratulations on that. I could have sworn Gene said TV.

Clifford It's not TV, it's advertising. It's this job I'm up for. In New York.

Patsy Here's to you—in *Rhode Island.*

Clifford The advertising job would pay really well and—

Patsy You don't need money, you're a kid.

Clifford *I* don't need anything, but Gene's so far behind on his credit cards—

Patsy Genie is always behind—

Clifford And Mom's not doing so well, lately. Her health . . .

Patsy, very sober all of a sudden, looks at Clifford.

Patsy Why do you think that is?

Clifford I'm sorry?

Patsy Clifford, when you were about to go away to college, the same thing happened.

Clifford It's a good thing I didn't go away to college. Can you imagine Genie handling the—

Patsy Clifford, listen to me: I don't care what you do, or where you go—just get the hell out of here.

Gene and Terry enter from bedroom door—a serious discussion underway. Clifford watches.

Gene Are you sure?

Terry It's been two months.

Gene Al knows someone who can take care of it.

Terry What?

Gene Patsy knows him too, he's very—

Terry (*horrified*) What are you talking about?

Gene Terry, you're not in East Boston anymore. You don't have to have a baby just because—

Terry You want to kill the baby? Our baby? OK, OK. It's OK.

Gene (*goes to her*) Terry—there's no baby yet.

Terry Oh my God. Oh my God. Oh my God.

Gene The sooner you take care of these things, the better it—

Terry Shut up. SHUT UP. SHUT UP. I don't want to kill the baby. I wanna have the baby. I don't care if he's a bastard. I want to keep the baby.

Gene Terry. Calm down. Get a—he won't be a bastard.

She calms down, a bit.

Gene Terry . . . we're getting married. OK? You're having the baby. It's OK. It's OK.

Terry You mean it?

Gene Sure.

Terry Oh, Genie.

They embrace, then she pulls back.

Terry You know, I've already been married.

Gene We'll do it 'til you get it right.

They kiss.

Gene We'll have a big wedding. I'll take care of everything. In the morning I'll talk to the caterers.

Terry We can't afford that. I can cook a lasagne—

Gene Terry, it's your wedding. We'll have a band, a cake, the works. This is going to be a night to remember.

Gene exits, to plan the celebration.

Terry (*to Clifford*) That was that. Two weeks later—

Clifford crosses downstage to Terry.

Clifford You made a lasagne.

Terry And we got married—

Clifford and Terry In the apartment.

Clifford helps her out of her robe—underneath, a wedding dress. She puts on shoes and a ring. He adds a corsage.

Terry I called Blimpie, Cupie, Fat Raffie, all my sisters, but they couldn't come . . . Afterwards, we went over to Charlie's to celebrate. Jonesy—he'd just gotten back from Vegas, danced with me while Gene sat in with the band. Everyone cut in all night long. Not to dance with me, but to sit in with Gene and the band.

Jonesy dances with Terry to a romantic ballad played by Gene.

Terry How come he doesn't dance with me? On his wedding night?

Jonesy Trumpet players don't dance.

Terry How come you dance?

Jonesy I play trombone. Patsy taught me. After she left Al . . . before she went back to her second husband.

Terry Bernie?

Jonesy No. Bernie was number three. She wouldn't leave me and Al for Bernie, because Bernie still plays. Greatest lead player in America. She went back to Stu—number two, if you're keeping score. Which in Patsy's case is almost impossible to do.

Terry Stu the foot doctor?

Jonesy (*to himself*) Stu the foot doctor. (*to Terry*) He used to be a good player. He came by 52nd Street one night, saw us all play. He started to cry. Ziggy looks at him and says: "Podiatrisht, heel thyshelf."

The ballad ends. Jonesy and Terry applaud. She motions for Gene to come join her. Instead, the band starts another tune: like "Daahoud," an up-tempo, undanceable, hard-bop number.

Terry How do you dance to this?

Jonesy You don't. You drink to it. That's another reason why jazz is dying. Let's go to the bar.

He steers her to the bar.

Terry I'll have a Shirley Temple.

Jonesy Terry, you marry a musician, you're gonna have to learn to drink hard stuff. Start with a Tom Collins.

Clifford serves Terry her first drink. She and Jonesy listen to the band.

Jonesy Gene sounds pretty good tonight.

Terry He told me never to tell anyone, but I think he sounds like Dizzy.

Jonesy In a way. Nicer tone than Dizzy. But he does those same long lines. Every solo has a beginning, middle, and end when he plays.

Terry Do you think he'll make it?

Jonesy Honey. He's made it. This is it.

Terry looks around, lets this sink in. Then:

Terry What about that record he did . . . with Charlie Barnett's band?

Jonesy He's a player Terry. He's not a hustler.

Terry But he played really well on it.

Jonesy Didn't he tell you what happened?

Terry No.

Jonesy Ask him about the review.

Terry (*to Clifford*) I had a nice time dancing with Jonesy. And the Tom Collins tasted kind of sweet. He bought me a few more, but then he had to leave—

Jonesy Got to see a man about some horse. I'll be back in half an hour.

Jonesy, who now needs a fix, has been compulsively scratching himself more and more throughout the scene. He walks out.

Clifford An hour went by, Charlie's was closing up, and Jonesy hadn't come back. Mom, who actually was a little psychic, told Gene:

Gene enters; she goes to him.

Terry He said he was going to see some horse or something. But I don't think the race tracks are still open. Maybe something happened to him at the track—

Gene Jonesy can take care of himself.

Al comes by.

Al Terry, best wishes. Genie, nice blowing tonight.

Ziggy comes by now, with Patsy on his arm. Al tenses up.

Ziggy (*in Al's face*) "Love ish lovelier . . . "

Patsy and Ziggy ". . . the sheventh time around."

Patsy Congratulations you kids.

Terry Have you guys seen Jonesy? I'm a little worried.

Patsy and Ziggy (*sing*) "If you knew Jonesy, like I knew Jonesy."

Al is not having fun.

Al Mazel tov.

Ziggy Geshundheit.

Al Screw you.

Al leaves. Ziggy looks at Patsy, she shrugs.

Patsy That stage should be over by now. Good-night everybody. Got to get home before the foot man wakes up for work.

Patsy exits. The others now walk out of Charlie's, too. End of the evening.

Terry (*to Clifford*) When we got outside, there was a police car parked across the street. Lights flashing. In the backseat, hands cuffed behind his back, was Jonesy.

Clifford (*to audience*) Mom spent the rest of her wedding night down in night court. Waiting.

Gene, Ziggy, and Terry watch and wait.

Terry How come they keep arresting Jonesy?

Ziggy Probably another bullshit crackdown caushe shome dealer misshed hish payoff.

Gene signals Ziggy to shut up.

Terry What's that have to do with Jonesy?

Gene Look, everything's going to be fine. We can post bail. I've got . . . fourteen bucks.

Ziggy Bragger.

Gene Terry, you don't have to hang around.

Terry (*her feelings hurt*) I'll stay.

They stand and wait for a while.

Terry Jonesy told me to ask you about the Charlie Barnett review.

Ziggy (*to Gene*) Try to bail a guy out, and he ratsh on you.

Gene tries to shush Ziggy.

Terry What happened?

Gene Didn't I tell you about this? I could have sworn I did.

Ziggy (*trying to distract*) You guysh shee what'sh going on in Budapesht?

   Terry glares at him, turns to Gene.

Terry What happened? And don't bullshit me.

Gene This big French jazz critic, Henri Arnaud, reviewed the album. He said that while the band sounded great, the trumpet solos were the best in the last decade.

Terry You're kidding. Why didn't you tell me? We should make photostats of the review. Send them out to club owners. To managers. Maybe Gene could get someone to . . . (*She notices they've gone silent*) You were lying to me? You fuck. Why—

Gene No I wasn't. Honest. They liked my playing.

Ziggy Liked it? They were nutsh about it.

Terry Why the fuck do you two lie to me like this?

Gene No one's lying, Terry. They liked my playing. Only problem is, they didn't know it was my playing. The guy screwed the credits up. He saw Bernie's name and everybody over there knows Bernie, because he's recorded with Miles and Gil and everyone else . . . It's no big deal.

Terry What's the magazine going to do about the mistake?

Gene I don't think they even know about it. You know, Bernie's a great player, and he deserves a good review.

Terry NOT FOR YOUR FUCKING SOLOS HE DOESN'T.

Gene LOWER YOUR VOICE. We're in a court for crissakes.

Terry YOU'VE GOT TO WRITE AND TELL THEM TO MAKE A CORRECTION.

Gene Calm down! That's not how it works. People in the business know my playing. I can't embarrass Bernie with a letter like that. (*patronizing*) What's the matter with you?

She is embarrassed now. After a long awkward moment, Ziggy sees:

Ziggy Joneshy. There he ish. JONESHY.

Gene JONESY!

Terry Oh my God! (*waves to him*) What's the matter with him?

Ziggy He probably needsh a fix, poor bashtard.

Terry What do we do?

Gene We could call Leon.

Ziggy Leon? Nobody'sh shpoken to him shince he moved to Boshton.

Gene He's a Harvard lawyer now. One call from a guy like that and the D.A. drops the charges.

Clifford Leon did what he could. It took two days because it was a weekend, but on Monday, Gene got in to see Jonesy.

Gene face-to-face with a badly beaten, strung-out Jonesy. Clifford watches intently.

Gene Anything I can do for you?

Jonesy Yeah, take my place.

Gene I'm serious—

Jonesy I'm all fucked up, Gene.

Gene What the hell happened?

Jonesy They wanted me to tell them who my dealer was. They said we'll give you a fix, if you tell us where you cop. They waved it in front of my face. I was dying for it. But I said, I can't trust you guys. Let me fix myself up first, then I'll tell you where I cop. So the bastards give me my stash, they'd already taken half of it for themselves, but I tie off, I shoot up, and I'm feeling no pain. OK wiseass, they say, tell us where this heroin comes from? I look them right in the eye and I tell them the truth: (*pause*) General MacArthur.

Gene looks at Jonesy, shakes his head.

Jonesy Well, how the hell do you think this stuff gets into the country? Anyway, this fuckin' bull goes nuts. He smacks me across the face. The other guys let him wail on me for a while before they pulled him off.

Jonesy opens his mouth, shows Gene his teeth.

Jonesy He broke three of my teeth Gene. (*starts to cry*) I don't know if I'll ever be able to play.

Jonesy staggers off as Gene moves to the living room. Terry knits. Clifford hands a pregnant, cigarette-smoking Terry her drink.

Clifford (*to audience*) They put him away . . . for eight years.

Terry (*to Clifford*) I wrote to him and sent care packages . . . I never heard from him.

Terry sits with Gene on the couch. She sips her Tom Collins. Clifford has, over the last few scenes, moved closer to the action. Now he stands in the living room and watches.

Terry (*to Gene*) You lied to me. When Jonesy was arrested the first time, it wasn't disorderly conduct, was it? It was for junk, wasn't it?

Gene I guess—I mean, he's not really a junkie junkie. More of an addict. He never misses a gig.

Terry He told me he doesn't have any gigs.

Gene It's a little slow right now. No one works in September—the Jewish holidays.

Terry Patsy says it's all over. Elvis. TV. L.A. Jazz is—

Gene Patsy is just pissed off because she can't get Al or Bernie or Ziggy to quit so she had to go back to Stu who spends his day touching people's feet. Is that what you want me to do?

Terry That's the same Bernie who got credit for your solos, isn't it?

Gene Most likely. So *what*.

Terry Why don't you send out those scripts you and Ziggy wrote?

Gene They're not ready.

Terry Do you want me to help?

Gene Honey, you can barely speak English; no one understands a word you say. How the hell are you going to help with the scripts?

Terry Fuck you.

Gene What? Oh don't get upset. I'm just saying. Ziggy and I went to college. We know what we're doing. As soon as those scripts are ready—they're going out.

Terry Do you have a gig for tonight?

Gene Not yet.

Terry and Gene Huh.

Gene It happens. What's the big deal.

Terry It's Saturday night.

Gene The Jewish holidays. No one's working.

Terry But it's Saturday night.

Gene Terry, I've got my twenty weeks in, I subbed at the Copa twice last week, what's so goddamn important about Saturday night. Jesus—a gig is a gig.

Terry You said if you ever weren't booked for a Saturday night, you'd quit the business.

Gene Oh, come on. I never said that.

She stares at him in disbelief, then anger.

Terry You lying motherfucker—

Gene Terry—

She walks away from him.

Terry You lying motherfucker—

Terry doesn't see Gene as he moves toward her.

Gene Terry, get a hold of your—

He is suddenly next to her. She bats him away.

Terry Get your hands off of me, Dominic—

Gene I'm Gene.

Terry I don't care who you are. All of you. Stay away. I can't take this bullshit. All of you lie. All of you fucking lie.

Gene STOP IT. Stop it.

She snaps back to reality. Calms a bit.

Terry What time is it?

Gene Nine.

Terry You have until midnight. If that phone doesn't ring, and you stay in the business, I'll fuckin' kill you. And I'll kill the baby.

She takes her drink and walks past Gene to the bedroom as Clifford sits.

Terry I swear to God, I'll kill you both.

She slams the bedroom door behind her.

END OF ACT I

ACT II

Same apartment, ten years later, with ten more years of inherited furniture, broken lamps, tchotchkes. Every surface is piled high; every inch of space below the couch or tables is crammed full as well.

Laid out on the couch is a very pale, dead Gene. Dressed in a tuxedo. Arms folded over his chest. The apartment is still. Dark.

Clifford She didn't kill him that night, and she didn't kill me. Three months later, the doctor slapped me and I was on the scene. Gene was playing Sinatra at the Copa. She was finally going to get to hear Frankie, live. But on the night she was supposed to go, she started to get contractions. Around the time Sinatra and my dad were playing "Someone to Watch Over Me," I was born. My dad never played Sinatra again, and to this day she's never seen him live. IT'S ALL MY FAULT. She was going to name me Francis Albert, but she was so pissed at me, she let Gene name me Clifford. After Clifford Brown. Now, Clifford Brown was a beautiful trumpet player, but Clifford has never been an easy name around the schoolyard. It might be OK for a forty-year-old shoe salesman, (*in the voice and/or manner of a child now*) but on a ten-year-old seventh grader, which is what I am by now, 'cause I skipped two grades and everyone thinks I'm a genius who's gonna save the family, it's kind of lame.

He crosses over to Gene, who doesn't stir.

NOTE: *In the next several scenes, when Clifford interacts with his family, he does so as a child; when he talks to the audience, he finds a middle ground between the manner of a child and the ironic detachment of the adult Clifford.*

Clifford (*to audience*) I liked bringing the guys from P.S. 145 to my apartment for their first time. I walk in with them, the house is dark—the house is always dark—and my father's lying like this. (*pointing to the corpse-like Gene*) Freaked 'em out every time. (*to Gene*) Dad, wake up! Club date. You told me to wake you at six.

Terry (*loud*) CLIFFORD! Clifford. My TV's fucked-up again. And check the oven.

Clifford In a minute Ma. Dad, wake up! (*looks at his father, who doesn't budge*) He can sleep through anything. But in this house, that's a good way to go.

Terry walks through now, in a robe. She is much older than she was. She's gained weight, and the last ten years have put a lot of mileage on her. She hands Clifford a glass.

Terry Here, your poor old mother wants a refill.

Clifford reluctantly takes the glass. Goes offstage to the kitchen.

Terry He fell asleep timing your labor pains, did I ever tell you that?

Clifford (*from kitchen*) A couple of thousand times, Ma.

Terry Don't be such a smart-ass. You know, it's because of you I never got to see Sinatra.

Clifford Really? (*hands her the drink*) I didn't know that. (*she walks to her offstage bedroom*) Dad, come on—time to eat.

Shakes his father a little. Gene comes to. He's older, but not nearly as worn as Terry.

Gene Where am I?

Clifford 1967. Saturday night. Club date. (*whispers*) Lester Lanin.

Gene Jesus, it's late. You should have woken me sooner. Lester hates it when I'm late.

Clifford And you hate being there at all. So it works out.

> *Clifford takes an oval tabletop from behind the couch and places it over the coffee table. Sets the table for dinner, then runs to the kitchen.*

Gene I do. I do hate him—did I tell you what Bernie does now? When Lester conducts, he doesn't conduct. You know, it bears no relation to the music, or any music, ever. Nobody in the band actually follows him. And he spends the whole night smiling and gladhanding his loyal, tone-deaf fans—those people couldn't swing if you hung them.

Clifford (*offstage*) Yeah, Dad, I know. But you're running late.

Terry (*offstage*) Clifford!

Clifford (*offstage*) Ma, it's almost done.

Gene So two months ago, Lester's facing the dance floor, Bernie signals, and the entire horn section skips a beat. One and Two and One THREE FOUR. Like that. Lester turns around. *He knows something's wrong,* but since we did it in unison, he can't figure out what happened. We did it six more times, just to see if he'd catch on.

Clifford (*returning*) That's great Dad. You've got like, ten minutes for dinner. Here's your salad.

Terry (*offstage*) Gene, don't forget to pick up cigarettes and some "medicine" on your way home.

Clifford hands Gene a pencil and an index card from Gene's trumpet case.

Gene I wrote it down.

Gene writes it down.

Clifford (*to audience*) He has to write everything down, even "Take a shower," or he'll forget. When my mom really wants to get back at him, she hides his cards, and he has no idea what to do, or where to be, or who he is.

Clifford runs to the kitchen. Gene finishes writing his note, now checks his wallet.

Terry (*offstage*) Get a fifth!

Gene I only have eight bucks, I'll pick up a pint.

Gene picks up his horn again. Before he can blow a note, she screams at him from the bedroom. It is a well-worn ritual.

Terry (*offstage*) Tomorrow's Sunday Gene. DON'T DO THIS TO ME. The stores are closed tomorrow.

Gene You ought to be able to get by on a pint.

Terry (*offstage*) DON'T DO THIS TO ME, GENE. I WAS ON DOUBLE SHIFTS ALL FUCKING WEEK. I want to goddamn relax on my day off.

Clifford returns with more plates, salad.

Gene (*looks at Clifford, whispers*) Just 'til Monday. When I can get to the bank.

Clifford nods. Reaches into his pocket. Gives his dad a five.

Terry (*offstage*) And don't take it from the kid.

Gene It's taken care of Terry.

Terry comes out of the bedroom, crosses to the kitchen.

Terry Did you say you're working Lester Lanin?

Gene Terry, would you let me practice. I'm late.

He picks up the horn, starts to finger the valves.

Terry (*from the kitchen*) You swore you wouldn't work for him again.

Gene I told you I'm not working with him, it's just a club date. I don't even know who the leader is. (*winks at Clifford*) Can I blow a couple of notes?

Terry (*from the kitchen*) You shouldn't be practicing at six o'clock. THE NEWS IS ON.

Clifford Ma. Do you need any help?

Terry (*from the kitchen*) It's too fucking late to practice.

Clifford Ma—we still have time to eat.

Terry (*from the kitchen*) No. Your father has to practice. He couldn't practice earlier. Has to wait until my programs are on.

Gene Terry, I just want to blow a few notes.

Now she comes out from the kitchen, with hunks of lasagne on plates.

Terry DON'T START IN WITH ME—ALL OF YOU. ALL OF YOU ARE IN THIS AGAINST ME.

"All of you" refers to Clifford and Gene, who are seated at the oval-topped coffee table. Which gives them little room to move. Terry—on fire—stands over the table. In one of her moods. Plates in hand.

Terry Oh sure—no one notices what your father does to me. But when I get upset—you all think Terry has gone crazy. He's gaslighting me.

Clifford Ma, watch out!

Terry tries to save the food and yell at the same time. She loses her balance, falls, and knocks over the oval table-top. Gene, in his tuxedo, instantly stands before anything stains him.

Terry Sure. Now you move. You motherfucker. Nothing gets you. Nothing gets you.

She runs through the living room to her bedroom. Slams the door. The whole apartment shakes. Father and son look at each other. Clifford gathers up what food he can.

Bedroom door opens.

Terry Enjoy your dinner—MOTHERFUCKERS!

She SLAMS the door. Gene shakes his head. Sits down. Continues to eat his salad. He and Clifford converse, uninterrupted by her blasts.

Clifford Dad, how come you didn't practice before your nap?

Gene, spaced out, blows on his salad fork.

Door opens.

Terry (*yelling from bedroom*) ASK YOUR FATHER!

SLAM.

Gene I went to move the car. It took a while to find a space— so when I came home—

Door opens.

Terry (*she's hysterical now*) Enjoy your macaroni, MOTHERFUCKERS.

SLAM.

Clifford What time did you leave to move the car?

Gene I don't know—four, four-thirty.

Clifford (*exasperated*) Dad, why do you do that? You
you can never find a space after four. It happens every ti

Gene I got hung up with some—

Clifford Yeah but Dad—you know she can't stand to hear
you practice. She was out all day, working, you could have—

Door opens.

Terry THAT'S RIGHT, MOTHERFUCKER.

*SLAM. The two of them sit there for a while. Eating
slowly.*

Terry (*offstage*) DOES ANYBODY LISTEN TO ME IN
THIS FUCKING FAMILY?

Gene Do we have a choice?

The door opens. She's got an empty cup in her hand.

Terry You better move your ass.

*She hurls the cup toward Gene—he ducks. It SMASHES
against the wall.*

Clifford (*to Gene*) She broke Bakelite. NICE MA, I didn't
think that was possible.

Gene tries to quiet Clifford.

Terry DON'T GET CUTE WITH ME.

Gene He wasn't getting cute with—

*She grabs his trumpet case, shakes it, AND THE HORN
GOES CRASHING TO THE FLOOR.*

Clifford Ma!

*Terry SLAMS the door behind her. Gene rushes to his horn
as if it were his child. Checks it carefully. It's OK. Now
tuxedo neat, trumpet case in hand:*

hanks for cleaning up. I'd better get
to eat something.

OK. See you later.

picks up.

ence) It's good for a family to have rituals.
was ours. Once, twice, three times a month. He'd screw
up. She'd flip out. He'd leave for work. I'd clean up. She'd
hide in the room. I'd bring her something to eat. She'd have a
few drinks. Fall asleep. He'd sneak in around four a.m. Every
once in a while she'd put furniture in front of the door. I'd
wait until she'd fall asleep, and I'd move it so he could get in.
If you got through the night without the cops coming, things
were usually fine in the morning.

Terry (*from the bedroom*) WHO are you talking to?

Clifford It's just me, Ma.

*Lights up now on the basement of the Metropolitan Club,
where Ziggy and Al arrive in matching powder blue tux
jackets.*

Al Man, I had a bitch of a time parking.

Ziggy Not me. I circled the island three timesh, drove over to
Newark, and took a shubway in.

Gene (*arriving late*) Hey, it's old home week.

Ziggy The turtle hash landed.

Al Hey, Gene Glimmer . . . (*looks at his watch*) You're almost
on time.

Ziggy I didn't know you were doing thish gig.

Gene Don't tell my wife. She thinks I'm a professional.

Ziggy How'sh she and the kid doing? Haven't sheen Terry
shince . . . the Cuban misshile crishish.

Gene The family? The family's great.

From upstairs, really bad 1967 rock music blares. They look up.

Al Man, how'd three guys like us end up on a gig like this?

Ziggy I think I'm retired and they forgot to tell me.

Gene I tell people I'm in the twilight of a mediocre career.

Gene takes out his horn. Starts to warm it up.

Al The bad news is that rock band upstairs is going to close out the night. So, no overtime for us.

Gene Good thing we're all rich.

Al The *bad* news is that the parents want us to play three sets straight for the old farts.

Gene Do they give us dinner?

Ziggy Theshe people? They won't even let ush pee.

Gene He's kidding, right?

Al Rules of the club. Musicians can't use the facilities that the guests are using. And the kitchen toilet is busted, but the busboys have worked out a deal with the coffee shop across the street. So—

Ziggy If we were black, they couldn't get away with thish.

Gene It's not as bad as the Copa, at least they're not charging us for water.

Ziggy The Copa: remember when Podel caught ush playing poker, and he ripped the card table out of the wall. Motherfucker couldn't shtand to shee a mushician have a good time.

Al Those were the days. We closed that together, didn't we?

Gene Are you kidding? Between us, I bet we closed every hotel, club, and ballroom in New York in the last 20 years.

They think about this for a second.

BACK AT HOME: Lights down on the guys and up on the apartment.

Clifford carries a dinner plate. Goes to the bedroom door.

Clifford Mom, I got dinner.

He puts the tray down. Slowly forces the door open. It's pitch black. Terry's not in her bed. He looks up and sees her now.

She is sitting on the windowsill. Her legs are off the ground. The window is wide open, and nine stories up.

Terry That's right. I know what I'm doing. He'll finally be sorry for what he's done to me.

Clifford sticks his head out the adjacent window to talk to her.

Clifford Ma.

She gets angry:

Terry Clifford, get your head back inside.

He does.

Clifford Mom—that's not a good place to sit.

Terry I won't be sitting here long.

Clifford I brought you dinner.

Terry He's not supposed to practice after six o'clock. Even the social worker told him that.

Clifford I know—

Terry (*suddenly maternal, worried*) Is the oven off? You have to be very careful with that oven. It's not safe. That's how my eyebrows got burned.

Clifford I know Ma—I remember—

Terry Fucking landlord. Your father wouldn't sue. We could have made a fucking fortune. But no—not your—

Clifford He felt really bad about screwing up tonight.

Terry Bullshit he did. You stay away from me. Don't try to con me out of this. I've been dead for fifteen years.

She starts to cry. Throws a tissue on the floor. He inches to the windowsill.

Clifford You saving these tissues for anything? Or can I throw them out?

Terry Is that supposed to be funny?

Clifford The ziti came out pretty good. But I think you may have overcooked the noodles—maybe it's a little . . .

Terry *Mushad?*

Clifford Maybe a little. What do you think? Why don't you come in from there and taste it?

Terry He hasn't taken me out to dinner in fifteen years.

Clifford Ma—you're too good a cook. Just taste it.

Terry Oh, Clifford.

Clifford Ma, please . . .

She turns to him and lets him gently pull her in from the sill.

Terry You shouldn't have to do this.

Clifford It's OK, Ma.

Terry He should do this. Not you.

She starts to cry. He holds her.

Clifford He's at work. It's OK, Ma. It's OK.

Back over to the Metropolitan Club where Ziggy, Al, and Gene have finished their sets. They're exhausted.

Ziggy Al, you all right?

Al He's a sadist.

Al is particularly beat.

Gene Fucking Lester does everything at the same tempo, how can he not know that trumpets need a rest once in a while?

Ziggy Theshe motherfuckersh know, they jusht don't give a shit. You heard what happened with the Circush? They come into Madishon Shquare Garden lasht month—add an extra show a day; and you know that booksh a killer: Shcreaming F'sh and G'sh all night. No breaksh. Firsht week, two trumpet playersh passh out, one hash a shtroke. The other getsh Bellsh Palshy.

Gene What did the union do?

Ziggy looks at Gene, incredulous.

Ziggy Thoshe motherfuckersh? They're all getting greashed.

Gene Yeah, but still. We pay dues.

Ziggy looks at him: Gene's hopeless. He tries Al.

Ziggy Finally, after a *third* kid bushts a vein in hish head, the NLRB people come in, and shay either the circush doublesh the hornsh, and shplits the book, or they have to shupply the trumpet shection with presshurized shuitsh.

Gene Well, I gotta get going. I promised the family I'd be home early.

Gene stands, they shake hands.

Al Hey, tell Terry I'm expecting a tray of lasagne for Christmas.

Ziggy And tell her I may want my lampsh back.

Gene If you can find them . . . you can keep 'em.

Gene starts to leave.

Al Wait a minute, I forgot to tell you: Jonesy's back in town. He's playing piano over at the Melody Lounge.

Gene Jonesy? His chops were just never the same after . . .

Ziggy After they bushted hish chopsh.

Al But dig this. He gave me this tape, it's going around. Brownie. Clifford. Some guys in Philly found this live recording of him, from the night he died.

Gene Not the "Night in Tunisia" solo?

Al pulls out a small, old-fashioned cassette player.

Al Just listen, you're not gonna believe this.

Al hits the play button on Clifford Brown's last recording of "A Night in Tunisia."

After a few notes:

Ziggy That'sh Clifford!

Now, chorus after inventive chorus. It is one thing to listen to this unbelievable recording. It is another thing entirely to watch three lifelong jazz trumpet players listen to this fabled lost masterpiece for the first time. Every turn Brownie takes causes them to shake their heads, laugh, murmur. They listen and react to every nuance of this solo with an intensity and passion that is otherwise not part of their lives.

Ziggy Can you believe—

Al Wait wait wait.

They are astonished by his level of musicianship. It brings tears to their eyes. The swiftness of their reactions, and the depth of their understanding of what Brownie is playing, tells us something about these three musicians as well. For all their joking and fucking up, they have a profound connection to their music, one they can only share with each other. Every time Ziggy and Gene think Clifford Brown has reached a musical climax, Al says:

Al Wait wait wait.

Brownie plays through the turnaround. Plays another chorus . . .

Gene in particular laughs at every quote within the solo. He smiles at the way Clifford threads his long melodic lines through the chords. Ziggy nudges Al to watch how Gene takes in the nuances. Each phrase builds on the one before it. Brownie takes another chorus, and the musicians are staggered.

Al Motherfucker. That is one motherfucker.

Gene is mute in ecstasy. Finally, Clifford all but ignites.

Ziggy That'sh it. I quit.

Freeze.

Back at the apartment:

Clifford tiptoes out of the bedroom. He goes to the TV, turns it on, lowers the volume down to zero. Then he goes to the couch, wraps himself in a blanket, and sits staring at the TV until Gene comes home.

Gene Hey kiddo. You're still up? I had the worst time finding a parking place. I must have clo '.ed three miles just looking for a space. But I finally found one that's good 'til Tuesday.

Clifford That's good Dad.

Gene Tough gig. Lester has no idea how to pace a band. Hey—the place looks good. Thanks for cleaning up.

Clifford Sure.

Gene How's she doing?

Clifford Fine.

Gene Is it OK for me to go in there?

Clifford She finally fell asleep.

Gene Do you think it's all right then?

Clifford I guess.

Gene Heard the wildest cassette tonight. Al brought it in. Clifford Brown—your namesake. I'd always heard that the night he died, you know he died in a car crash—

Clifford I know. With Richie Powell. Ten years ago.

Gene He was only twenty-five. And he was clean. Has it been that long?

Clifford It was right before I was born, that's why you named me—

Gene You're not ten. Are you ten already?

Clifford Dad . . .

Gene Wow.

Gene disappears into space for a moment. Clifford waits.

Gene Ten years. Hmmn. They said the night he died, he played as if he knew he was going to die. That he must've known, because anyone who was there, it was in the back of a music store in Philly, people who were there said it was . . . they never heard anything like it in their lives. People have talked about that solo like it's one of the lost wonders of jazz.

Well—it turns out some guy recorded it on wire, and Al got a tape of it. You're not going to believe this . . .

Goes to the cassette player. Puts it in.

Gene His last night on earth. Dig this—

"A Night in Tunisia" comes on. Clifford listens with his father. They shake their heads in awe at what they hear. Clifford laughs at the same spots Al and Ziggy did. He has inherited his father's understanding of the music. They get so caught up in the playing that neither notice Terry as she emerges from her dark room.

She punches the music off. Gene and Clifford look up, terrified.

Terry Where the fuck have you been?

Gene It went overtime. You know these things.

Terry You went out with the guys. Had fun. I'm home alone and you went out with the guys. Was Patsy there?

Gene Terry, please—

Terry She always had a thing for you.

Gene Terry, Patsy had a thing for everyone.

Terry Don't get smart with me. Did you bring me my bottle?

She starts for his trumpet case. Gene grabs it before she can get to it. He opens the trumpet case. Hands her a bottle.

Terry What is this?

Gene Sherry—it's what they had—

Terry I don't drink sherry—

Gene You don't drink that?

Terry Not for two years.

Gene What difference does it make, booze is booze Terry.

Terry What the fuck is that supposed to mean?

Gene (*to Clifford*) Poison is poison.

Terry And you're so fucking clean, Gene. A monk. Gene's so sweet. Gene is so clean. Bullshit. Fifteen years of your bullshit and lies: "It's just slow right now. Wait until this record comes out. Every TV station will have a band. We'll go on vacation next year. You shouldn't be tired, you're a waitress, not a doctor. We'll get our own furniture." YOU AND YOUR FUCKING LIES. (*to Clifford*) Your father hasn't touched me in ten years. I'VE HAD IT. DO YOU HEAR ME. ALL OF YOU.

> *She takes the sherry and pours it over the living room. She soaks the rug. She starts to light her cigarette.*

> *She looks at the match. Then at the rug. She throws the match on the rug.*

Clifford Ma!

Terry Francis, you stay out of this.

> *She lights another, and another. Flings them at the rug, at Gene; she fails to start a fire and finally throws the whole box of matches to the floor.*

Terry Get away from me. Get away from me. Goddamn it. You got the wrong booze. If you'd gotten bourbon this whole fucking place would be on fire by now.

> *Terry breaks down in a wail of tears. Clifford steps downstage; he is no longer a child.*

> *Over Clifford's monologue, we hear Gene playing "Willow Weep for Me."*

Clifford (*now an adult again, to audience*) I had to call an ambulance that night. They came and took Mom away. She

71

talked herself out in a couple of weeks. After a while, she started to call them herself, when she was losing it. If they didn't come fast enough, she'd call again and tell them—

Terry 10–13, 10–13! Officer Down! *OFFICER DOWN!* (*to Clifford*) That'll bring'em in a hurry.

Clifford (*to audience*) It went on like this, for years. Through high school, through college. And I never got away.

Terry and Gene circle each other warily in the living room, then exit.

Clifford I kept hoping they'd be like old generals at war, finally realizing they're all they have; that their memories of how they tried and failed to kill each other would eventually give them a bond. It didn't work that way. Even after college, when I finally moved out, the farthest I could get was across the street. I was still on duty.

A phone rings. Clifford crosses to phone.

Clifford The four a.m. phone call. The second the phone rings, you know you're in for a long night. And you've been trained since birth to handle it. (*into phone*) "Yes officer. You've found my mother naked on Amsterdam Avenue? Uh-huh. She wants you to put her on a bus so she can join a convent in Montana? OK. Well, don't do that. What emergency room is she in? Fine. I'll be right up. Thank you."

Clifford hangs up the phone and crosses to his mother in an emergency room. She's completely wrecked.

Clifford You OK?

Terry What the fuck are you doing here?

Clifford I don't know.

Terry I never should have married your father—

Clifford It's a little late Ma.

Terry Motherfucker booked a club date on our anniversary. How could he *forget* our anniversary?

Clifford (*to audience*) She has a point.

Terry WHO ARE YOU TALKING TO?

Clifford Sorry, Ma.

Terry I have had it with all of you motherfuckers. I want to go to a convent. In Minnesota—

Clifford I thought it was Montana.

Terry It's one of those "M" states in the middle there, Clifford. Don't give me a hard time. I told the bastards to just put me on a bus. But they *had* to call you.

Clifford It's OK. I was up anyway.

Terry (*She starts to cry.*) I'm sorry. Clifford. I've lost it again, haven't I? (*Clifford doesn't answer*) It's his fault.

Clifford He tries Ma.

Terry You know the worst part, once you've been in a nuthouse? Every time something feels wrong, you don't know—is it wrong, or are you going crazy again . . . you just don't know.

She starts to sob. Stands over Clifford now.

Terry Make sure I get a roommate who smokes, Clifford.

Clifford I'll see what I can do.

Terry I used to tell your father, it wasn't right, that you had to do this. You know what your father said: "That's why you have kids Terry, so they'll take care of you." You never should have saved me Clifford. I've been dead for thirty years anyway.

Terry exits.

Clifford (*to audience*) I went to work; I was two hours late. No one noticed. I spent the morning writing ads. At lunchtime, I went into a stairwell and cried. For the first time in twenty years. I finished the afternoon, like nothing happened.

Clifford, now with Gene, who's more spaced-out than usual.

Clifford Couldn't you tell that she was losing it, before she—

Gene How can you tell? It's irrational.

Clifford You ran out of insurance. They want to send her upstate.

Gene She'll talk her way out of it.

Clifford They won't let her come home if you're here.

Gene You know, she drinks.

Clifford *Really?*

Gene After she flipped out, I found bottles all over the place.

Clifford What?

Gene Things just got . . . the boozing, the flip outs—I just thank God it started after you left home.

Clifford Are you *serious?*

Gene It didn't get bad 'til the last couple of years.

Clifford Dad, you're nuts. That's just not . . . she's had a drinking problem since I can remember.

Gene Clifford, I think I would know that.

Clifford I DON'T.

Gene (*changing the subject*) So what do you want to do?

74

Clifford What do *you* want to do? She's your wife.

Gene She won't talk to me when she's like this. She's completely irrational. You know that.

Clifford Why does it have to be up to me?

Gene You're the son. She's your mother. Who else is there?

Clifford Dad, what the fuck is your problem, she's your wife. SHE'S YOUR WIFE and if we don't do something, she's gone. Do you get it? *DO YOU UNDERSTAND WHAT'S GOING ON?*

   Gene spaces out.

Clifford Are you listening to me?

Gene There's no reason to get upset. You always figure something out. You're the RED CROSS.

   Gene stares into space. There is a long, awkward pause.

Clifford OK, get your horn, you're out.

Gene I'm sorry?

Clifford Get your fuckin' horn, and get out.

Gene What are you talking about?

Clifford Dad, she can't live with you. She can't get a place on her own. I'm not letting them send her upstate. You're out. It's over.

Gene Clifford.

Clifford It's over. As of tonight. Call Ziggy. Call Al. I don't give a fuck. Call someone. You're out of here.

   He packs the horn, gives it to Gene.

Clifford Dad, she's coming, you're going. You two are done.

Gene I don't think it's that bad.

Clifford You don't think, Dad. You don't know. YOU DON'T HAVE A FUCKING CLUE. (*he pushes the case into Gene*) You don't have a fucking clue.

Gene stares at Clifford, completely in shock. Gene walks out. Clifford steps forward.

Clifford (*to audience*) Before that night, I had never yelled at my father. And yelling at him . . . if my mom couldn't get through to him in thirty years, I wasn't going to either.

That night, at midnight, I drove him over to Ziggy's. I don't think he had any idea what was going on. It was like moving a cat.

In two weeks, Terry got out. I took her home, stayed with her the first couple of nights. After I left, she went right back to drinking.

Meanwhile, Ziggy told me he and Gene were going at it pretty good down in Hell's Kitchen.

Gene and Ziggy enter, face off.

Ziggy Did you get bananash?

Gene No, I got hung up at the bank . . . there was a line. Then by the time I went to move the car . . .

Ziggy *Why* do you go to the bank at three p.m. on a Friday?

Gene I always go to the bank on Friday.

Ziggy Fridaysh' payday, Genie. For shtraight people. It'sh a mob shcene.

Gene Is that true? I always wondered why it was crowded, but—everyone gets paid on Friday?

Ziggy That'sh it—

Gene (*sees Ziggy leaving*) Where are you going?

Ziggy It'sh rush hour, I'm going to go get a few sheats on the shubway! (*to Clifford*) I don't know how your old lady put up with him.

Ziggy and Gene exit.

Clifford (*to audience*) She didn't . . . But she couldn't make it without him either. She kept drinking for a few more years, finally fell into a coma. Liver shut off. Lung cancer. The works. Naturally, she came out of it. Quit drinking, denies ever having had a drinking problem. And still smokes three packs a day. She still makes a decent lasagne. And Genie . . . I haven't seen him in five years . . .

He looks to the offstage bandstand. "I Remember Clifford" plays. We're back to 1985 at the bar of the Melody Lounge.

Clifford He looks the same, and . . . he still plays a pretty horn . . .

Patsy rejoins him.

Patsy He's playing "I Remember Clifford."

Clifford Genie on a ballad, break your heart every time.

Patsy How are you? Are you happy?

Clifford (*never been asked this before*) What?

Patsy Are you happy?

Clifford I'm always fine.

They listen to Gene's solo.

Patsy He plays it every time.

Clifford (*amazed*) He does?

Clifford and Patsy listen as Gene finishes the last few notes of "I Remember Clifford." When he finishes playing, they applaud. She takes him across the stage to the booth.

Gene (*offstage*) Thank you folks. That was "I Remember Clifford." We'd like to welcome you to the Melody Lounge. We're going to take a short break so you all can catch your breath, and we'll be right back.

Clifford and Patsy applaud again as Ziggy, and Gene, trailing behind, cross over to the bar. Gene walks right past his son, does not see him.

Clifford (*standing*) Dad.

Ziggy Turtle, your shon ish here.

Clifford Yo, Dad—

Gene stares for a second, at last sees his son—six feet away.

Gene Hey . . . Clifford.

Clifford Yeah. I . . . I was going to call you, before I—to let you know, but . . . You sounded good.

Gene Not any more.

Ziggy tries to sneak by them to Patsy in the booth. Gene collars him.

Gene Hey, Ziggy, Al brought in a tape last week—air-check from Thornhill's band—I guess I used to blow . . . back then.

Ziggy (*on the way to Patsy's booth*) Oh bullshit—you shtill shound good. (*to Clifford*) He'sh shtill driving me crazy.

Ziggy goes to the booth. Gene and Clifford have another awkward moment alone together.

Clifford How come Al's on drums?

Gene He had a mini-stroke, so . . .

Clifford I'm sorry—

Gene There's many fewer high notes on the drums . . . Did you see Patsy? (*turns to the booth*) Hey, Patsy, the *k-i-d* is here.

Gene leads Clifford over to the booth as Al and Jonesy join Patsy and Ziggy there. The gang is all there, but much the worse for wear.

Patsy I know—old home week.

Al (*showing the effects of his stroke*) Gene—I told Patsy we'd let her sing with the band once the place is completely empty.

Ziggy Do you all remember Genie'sh boy?

Jonesy Is that Frankie? Jesus Christ. I knew you when your dick was this big.

He holds up one third of his pinky. Everyone laughs.

Ziggy Hish name ish Clifford, after Clifford Brown.

Jonesy It was supposed to be Francis Albert, but then the night you were born—

Clifford I know the story.

Jonesy I'll bet you do—Hey, how's Terry doing?

Clifford (*deflecting, to Patsy*) How's Stu?

Patsy He died on me a year ago.

Clifford That's a bitch. I'm sorry to hear it.

Patsy He was going to start playing again, after he retired.

Al You guys heard Bernie is in the hospital? In Germany. Cancer.

Jonesy No. I didn't know that.

Al Yeah, he's been living over there for years. Some teaching gig.

Jonesy Who else died? (*to Clifford*) It's our favorite game.

Ziggy (*trying to give Gene and Clifford some privacy*) Uh fellash, let'sh a—the shooner we go back in, the—

Patsy What should I sing?

Clifford My mom had a request.

Al and Ziggy "Just My Fucking Luck"?

Clifford Nope.

Jonesy and Patsy "Why Was I Born"?

Clifford Bingo.

Ziggy Fellash—Patshy—two tunesh in, your on.

The guys head up onto the bandstand. Gene, the slowest, lags behind. Clifford stops him.

Clifford Dad . . . (*they look at each other*) It's been a while.

Gene You're busy. Work. You're job's—

Clifford I quit.

Gene You quit? Are you gonna be able to collect—

Clifford I'm gonna go west—work on the . . . painting stuff. I was hoping you'd look in on her once in a while.

Gene thinks about this.

Gene You were always good with those collages you know.

Clifford can't believe his father noticed.

Clifford Huh?

Gene Not just me—your mother always thought that's what you were gonna do.

Clifford It's just cut and paste . . . see how it goes. How've you—

Gene You'll be fine—keep your nut small, pay your dues, as long as you have a place to paint . . .

They look at each other.

Gene How's she look?

Clifford OK, so-so . . . she gave me some lasagne, to give you.

Gene (*thinks about Terry*) Terry. She . . . (*Gene is suddenly overwhelmed. An instant later he seals it up.*) OK kiddo. Thanks for . . .

They have an awkward choice: to hug good-bye or to shake hands. They stop. Start. Finally, Gene just turns and goes up toward the bandstand.

Clifford Dad—"Why Was I Born"?

Gene I'll play it. Two tunes in. Good to see you kiddo.

Clifford If you think of it, call her in the morning, say thanks.

Gene heads up onto the bandstand.

Clifford He's not going to remember to call her. But I have to ask, same way I ask Mom to come and hear him play.

Lights up on Terry in her bedroom doorway, smoking a cigarette, alone.

Terry Leave your poor old lady alone Clifford. I'm not going over there to hear that rat-bastard play. Thirty years he never took me out. (*she stops*) And besides, if I hear him play—I get all . . . (*she starts to cry*) You go. Godspeed, caro figlio.

Lights out on Terry.

Clifford So long, Ma. (*to audience*) Like I said: No clean breaks.

Clifford crosses to the bar, listens to Gene onstage as he starts to play "It Never Entered My Mind." We see a silhouette of Gene playing behind a scrim.

Clifford When he's up there, blowing, he's totally in touch with everything that's going on around him. Ziggy bends a note, he echos it instantly. A car horn sounds outside, he puts it into his solo, or harmonizes under it, a second later. I used to wonder how he could sense everything while he was blowing, and almost nothing when he wasn't. Now I just wonder how many more chances will I have to hear him blow. If I have kids . . .

These guys are not even an endangered species anymore. It's too late. There are no more big bands, no more territory bands. No more nonets, or tentets. No more sixty weeks a year on the road. No more jam sessions 'til dawn in the Cincinatti Zoo. When they go, that'll be it.

No one will even understand what they were doing. A fifty-year blip on the screen. Men who mastered their obsession, who ignored, or didn't even notice, anything else. They played not for fame, and certainly not for money. They played for each other. To swing. To blow. Night after night, they were just burning brass. Oblivious.

The lights come down on the Melody Lounge as the music comes up.

THE END